Tom Brady: The Inspiring Story of One of Football's Greatest Quarterbacks

An Unauthorized Biography

By: Clayton Geoffreys

Visit my website at www.claytongeoffreys.com
Cover photo by Keith Allison is licensed under CC BY 2.0 / modified from original

Table of Contents

Foreword

Few players can ever say ESPN created a documentary on the players drafted before themselves. Tom Brady is one of, if not the only individual who can say this. His legacy as a quarterback is so deeply cemented at this point that ESPN produces documentaries reliving the day when teams passed on Brady before the New England Patriots drafted him. The rest is history. Brady has since won multiple championships and led his team to impressive clutch victories through the years. Despite recent controversy, the overall career of Tom Brady is one of intense perseverance from a player who loves the game and loved even more to prove others wrong. Thank you for purchasing *Tom Brady: The Inspiring Story of One of Football's Greatest Quarterbacks*. In this unauthorized biography, we will learn Tom's incredible life story and impact on the game of football. Hope you enjoy and if you do, please do not forget to leave a review! I read every review to improve revised editions of all of my works.

Also, check out my website at claytongeoffreys.com to join my exclusive list where I let you know about my latest books and give you goodies!

Cheers,

Clayton Geoffreys

Introduction

Tom Brady has accomplished a lot in 15 seasons in the National Football League. He was the starting quarterback for the New England Patriots and took over for the legendary Drew Bledsoe. He was the Most Valuable Player in the NFL for multiple seasons, is one of three quarterbacks in history with four Super Bowl championship victories, and had several appearances in the league's annual Pro Bowl game. Let us also throw in some major motion picture appearances, a few hit television shows like *Saturday Night Live* and *Family Guy*, and being considered by many as one of the faces of today's NFL.

With all of the positives in the past 15 years, there has been recent news and controversies surrounding Brady and the Patriots organization which have led some to question the integrity of Brady's legacy.

The Deflate-Gate controversy questions whether Brady had an unfair advantage throwing with under-inflated footballs during New England's 45-7 win against the Indianapolis Colts in the 2015 AFC Championship game. Such controversy puts to question how the game would have played out differently otherwise and possibly changed the outcome of Super Bowl XLIX where New England defeated the Seattle Seahawks, the defending champions from the previous season, 28-24. However, others suggest that Brady's numbers would not have made a difference in the grand scheme of events since the Colts only scored seven points in a game where the Patriots had three touchdowns from their running back LeGarrette Blount.

Then there was the Patriots' Spygate scandal that accused head coach Bill Belichick of coordinating videotaping efforts of hand signals used by opposing defenses. The signals were later on passed to Brady who was then able to make an audible – changing the play on the field – based on what he saw in the defensive set up and signals during the game. Still, the league has not taken away any of the five Vince Lombardi trophies the organization has won since 2001, nor have they banned anyone from the game. This is a similar case to that of Pete Rose, who bet on baseball while acting as manager of the Cincinnati Reds from 1984 to 1989.

If we look at his career through the current scope of NFL officials, Brady is one of the most consistent quarterbacks in the NFL. He is the only one with five championship rings – better than Terry Bradshaw (Pittsburgh Steelers, 1970-1983) and Joe Montana (San Francisco 49ers/Kansas City Chiefs, 1979-1994) – one of Brady's heroes while growing up as a youth athlete in Southern California. During his childhood, Brady dreamed of being among names like Montana in the NFL history books, but it seemed unlikely until he left his family's home in California for the University of Michigan, where it took some time before he got a chance to show his abilities.

In two years as a starter, Brady was able to win two bowl games with a 20-5 record for the Wolverines. When it came to the 2000 NFL

Draft, he fell to the sixth round and was expected when he was placed fourth on the New England Patriots' depth chart in his rookie season. But all that he needed was a chance, which came when long-time Patriots star Drew Bledsoe went down with a serious injury. Since then, Brady has won an average of 12 games per season, including a historic 16-0 regular season and multiple individual awards.

There may be doubters because of the recent controversy, mostly from those who are not within the New England Patriot fan base, but such doubt from others has never stopped Brady. It did not stop him when he was growing up, and the attention was on the athleticism of his three older sisters, not when he could not make the freshman team in high school his first year, nor when he struggled to get playing time in Ann Arbor, Michigan. Looking at his performances throughout his 15-year career wearing the red, white, and blue uniform with the now recognizable number 12 on the front and back, he has always bounced back from adversity and has put up some of the best numbers by any quarterback in the league.

While some question those numbers, it is hard to argue how good Brady has played each year and not just having one or two highlight seasons that inflate his averages. Despite the concerns, Brady has proven that he belongs in the conversation as one of the greatest NFL quarterbacks of all time, and he will likely remain there for an extended period after his eventual retirement down the road.

With five Vince Lombardi trophies at home – along with international model Gisele Bundchen as the often dreamt of a trophy wife, three children, and millions of dollars through various endorsement deals – Tom Brady has just about everything any man could want. Whether you are a die-hard Patriots fan who loves him like a sports deity, or hate him because you belong to a rival fan base that has been tormented by the man wearing the red, white, and blue number 12 jersey, there is no denying that Brady has had one of the most successful careers in the NFL. Remarkably, after the 2017-18 season, he will have been in the NFL for 18 years unless he signs another extension to continue beyond his contract's final season.

Whenever his career comes to an end, Brady is likely to be a first-ballot inductee into the Pro Football Hall of Fame in Canton, Ohio. He is one of the most consistently reliable quarterbacks no matter the supporting cast of wide receivers, tight ends, running backs, or lineman. He is currently throwing for more than 50,000 passing yards, nearly 400 touchdown passes, and a 95.9 career quarterback rating over 209 appearances with the New England Patriots. And do not forget the four NFL championships, three times named the most valuable player of the Super Bowl – most recently in Super Bowl XLIX in a 28-24 win over the Seattle Seahawks on February 1, 2015, at the University of Phoenix Stadium in Glendale, Arizona. He also has ten appearances in the NFL Pro Bowl game and is a member of the NFL's 2000s All-Decade Team.

Chapter 1: Childhood and Early Life

Nothing special happened when Tom Brady was born on August 3, 1977, as the youngest child of Galynn and Tom. He grew up in San Mateo, California — which lies in the middle of Silicon Valley near the San Francisco Bay – as the only boy out of four children and the youngest after Maureen, Nancy, and Julie. Every member of the Brady household was into playing sports, and his sisters would play just about everything that involved being active – softball, soccer, and basketball, to name a few. Young Tom was considered a supportive little brother and attended all of their games.

The oldest, Maureen, was a star on the softball diamond as a pitcher and even earned a spot on the U.S. Junior Olympic team at age 17 and would eventually earn a college scholarship to play at Fresno State University. She would become an All-American ace in the softball pitching circle and made two appearances in the College World Series before graduating in 1995. She ended her career with the Bulldogs, ranked sixth in appearances (126), eighth in games started (105), eight in wins with an 80-31 record, ninth in complete games (94), and has the school's seventh-longest consecutive scoreless inning streak at 35.

The youngest of the three sisters, Nancy, was a softball star in her right and earned a scholarship to the University of California-Berkeley before she would decide to pursue other collegiate studies. Julie was a standout soccer player at St. Mary's College of Southern California in Moraga, where she played from 1992 to 1995. An interesting note about Julie is that she married famed Boston Red Sox infielder Kevin Youkilis in 2012, according to a Boston Herald report.

The four children would attend each other's games – whether it was softball for Maureen or Julie, or Tom's baseball catching. Eventually, he would catch the competitive spirit that surrounded the house – the Brady who would eventually become a household name after his three older sisters made their names in the area and went on to Division I athletic programs.

Brady would begin playing football while attending St. Gregory's Catholic School in San Mateo. His earliest experiences were playing flag and touch football at recess and after school – playing quarterback of course. As a young football fan, he would watch the San Francisco 49ers and watched Joe Montana and Steve Young – both were pioneering Hall of Fame caliber careers of their own. In fact, one of Brady's earliest memories was a toddler attending the 1981 NFC Championship Game at Candlestick Park in San Francisco, California. It was the game where Montana threw "the Catch" to Dwight Clark to help the 49ers defeat the Dallas Cowboys, 28-27 on January 10, 1981 – a memory he recalled during the press conference of a 2011 game in Oakland.[i] In fact, most of his childhood involved going to San Francisco games while he looked up to Montana during his 13 successful seasons leading the 49ers before being traded to the Kansas City Chiefs in 1993. But during his time in the red and gold, Montana led the team to four Super Bowl championships and finished his career with 40,551 passing yards, 273 touchdowns against 139 interceptions, and a total record of 117-47.[ii]

Young would take over as the full-time starting quarterback in 1992 and would win a Super Bowl trophy of his own after defeating the in-state rival San Diego Chargers 49-26 on January 29, 1995 at Joe Robbie Stadium. Young would throw for 325 yards and six touchdown passes, including three to fellow Hall of Fame player Jerry Rice.

In addition to watching two great quarterbacks play for the 49ers, Brady was also going to a number of youth football camps that were hosted by the College of San Mateo. It was there where the young Brady learned how to throw from Tony Graziani, who played briefly in the NFL with the Atlanta Falcons and Cleveland Browns before going to the Arena Football League.[iii]

High School Years

There were never any indications early on that Brady had a chance to become one of the best to ever play in the National Football League, or even step out of the shadows cast by his sisters' athletic achievements. Eventually, Brady would play football as a freshman at Junipero Serra High School, a Catholic all-boys school in San Mateo, which also produced all-star athletes like baseball's Barry Bonds and football's Lynn Swann – each with successful careers in their respective sports.

Still, Brady would not take a snap during his freshman season – not on the varsity squad, junior varsity, and not even the freshman team that went winless; they also never scored a single touchdown in the fall of 1991[iv]. This was one of the earlier moments where Brady showed his focus on being better. For one of his classes in the ninth grade, he wrote that he was not going to forget the disappointment of being on the bench. There was confidence that he wrote about how his sisters, who grew up the well-known collegiate athletes in their respective sports, were going to be known as "Tom Brady's sisters" – and that he was going to do everything he could to become a household name. Back then, people thought it was funny. But no one dared tell someone that their goals were impossible. Back then, no one imagined the road to football stardom that Brady would take that started back at Junipero Sierra High School.

It was just a matter of Brady improving his foot speed, which was not the strongest part of his quarterback abilities. There was never a problem with his arm, but he moved slower than molasses. Despite that, he was still considered by one of the best natural athletes, according to his high school coaches. Whether it was after school, after practices during the season, or after finishing his homework, he would make sure he went to the nearby health club to get a good workout in. Over the years, Brady made some improvements that involved making the necessary changes to his throwing mechanics and foot agility, and he started to make strides in his overall football game despite the fact that most people thought his future was going to be in baseball. That is not what Brady wanted, and he strived to be a great quarterback with his first opportunities coming during his sophomore year of high school. As a sophomore, he would get his chance when the player ahead of him on the depth chart did not try out for football. His first throw as a quarterback came during his first high school scrimmage – a 60-yard touchdown. That first pass in high school would set the tone for his success for the next two decades.

Brady would become the starting quarterback for the Padres in his junior year and flourished in those two seasons on varsity. Throughout his time at Junipero Serra, Brady totaled more than 3,500 passing yards and 32 touchdowns while completing more than half of his pass attempts with an 11-9 record over two seasons. He was among the top three quarterbacks in school history for career completions (219), completions in a season (129) and touchdown passes (33). He also tied another top quarterback in the high school for the most completions in a game with 22.[v] His best game was during his senior year against Sacred Heart Cathedral where he threw for 331 yards, and Brady had a chance with a game-winning drive. However, he was on the opposing seven yard line with seconds left, only to throw an interception that was returned 101 yards for a pick-six touchdown.[vi] It was considered one of the toughest losses Brady ever suffered in his young athletic career, which was the biggest loss of his 11-9 high school career as Serra High School would finish 6-4 in the 1993 season and 5-5 in the 1994 season. But despite that, he was still the football team's most valuable player in his senior season.

He was also named not only to the all-league team but also on similar teams featuring the best in the San Mateo County and the northern half of California.

There were not a lot of college scouts looking at him initially during his sophomore season, which is when his father decided to make an investment. Both father and son worked together to make about 60 highlight tapes of the Serra quarterback's high school career; the cost alone cost about $2,000.[vii] According to media reports that inquired, Brady and his dad sent the tape to many schools around the state like Stanford University, St. Mary's College, and the University of California-Davis. They even decided to send a video to the University of Michigan. Overall, more than 50 different schools received the video of a young Tom Brady who showed plenty of drive to want to succeed[viii]. Therefore, more schools started to come out during his senior season. The final list of schools that were showing the most interest led to local schools like the University of Cal-Berkley, the University of California – Los Angeles (UCLA) and the University of Southern California (USC); all three were part of the Pacific-10 Conference. The other two schools outside the West Coast who also showed interest were the University of Illinois and the University of Michigan, both from the Big Ten Conference. All were big programs that were also going to give Brady a great college degree if the football career did not work out in the end.

However, there were also baseball teams that were wishing to court the two-sport athlete from Serra High School. Brady was also a star catcher for the school's baseball team, including a game against their main rival Bellarmine College Preparatory School, out of San Jose, California, where he had two home runs, the second of which landed on the roof of a school bus parked beyond the right field fence. The numbers were so good that he was offered a minor league contract with the Montreal Expos after being drafted as a catcher in the 18th round of the 1995 MLB Draft. So with college football teams and a chance to play professional baseball both calling Brady, what was he going to choose?

Rather than test his luck in an attempt to make it to Major League Baseball, Brady decided to accept a scholarship to play football for the University of Michigan, and by the time he graduated from high school in 1995, Brady was bound for Ann Arbor, Michigan. In retrospect, as we reflect on the events that followed both in Michigan and later in the greater Boston area, it is safe to say that committing to football was the right decision. Granted, the first thing Brady was going to have to adjust to was the difference in the fall weather between San Mateo, California – which usually keeps a low around the 40s from September through January – and the much colder Ann Arbor, Michigan. The campus would present Brady with temperatures that would drop to below freezing near the end of the year.

Chapter 2: College Years at the University of Michigan

After being one of the best high school quarterbacks in the Silicon Valley area, Brady enrolled at the University of Michigan in the fall of 1995 and found himself seventh on the depth chart. That featured names like Brian Griese, who was a sophomore at the time, and fellow freshman Scott Dreisbach. First-year head coach Lloyd Carr looked at his quarterback situation and made the decision to redshirt him so that he would have a chance to develop for a year without losing a year of eligibility.[ix] The Wolverines still had success with a 9-4 record Texas A&M, 22-20, in the Alamo Bowl on December 28, 1995.[x]

But similar to being benched by the freshman coaches at Serra High School in the fall of 1991, Brady was going to use that as motivation to prove that he belonged at the campus in Ann Arbor, Michigan, and that he was worthy of being a quarterback at the NCAA Division I level. In fact, one of his teammates would tell people that he often spent most of his time not in class or practice at Michigan's Schembechler Hall, which was home to the football team's weight room.[xi]

Even though he was no longer at the bottom of the depth chart, Brady still found himself low on the quarterback totem pole behind second-stringer Brian Griese and the returning starter Scott Dreisbach after returning from a right thumb and wrist injury the year before. With that in mind, the third-string quarterback was going to get his time to shine at different times over the season. While Brady watched from the sideline, Dreisbach led Michigan to an 8-3 record during the regular season before losing to the Alabama Crimson Tide, 17-14, in the Outback Bowl on January 1, 1997. He still made appearances in two games, but only threw a total of five passes with only three completions for only 26 yards and one interception. The stats were accumulated during garbage time when the game was already in hand, like the 38-9 rout of the UCLA Bruins on September 28, 1996, and the 44-10 rout of the Minnesota Golden Gophers on October 26, 1996. It probably did not surprise anyone, but Brady would spend the offseason still working out when he was not in class to continue to improve before the fall of 1997.

Brady sat on the bench behind Brian Griese, who led the Wolverines to an undefeated season and would defeat the Washington State Cougars 21-16 in the Rose Bowl and eventually the National Championship with the top rank of all teams in the nation. Brady went 12 out of 15 of his throws for 103 yards in passing that year when he came in four games when Michigan was well ahead [xii]

During this time, Brady hired a sports psychologist to assist in working through frustrations and anxiety of not being a starting quarterback, possibly a side effect of the competitive spirit he had growing up and wanting to reach a level beyond his sisters' sports accomplishments. There was even a moment that he thought about transferring to the University of California at Berkeley – which was only about 35 miles away from his hometown as opposed to the much longer trip of more than 2,300 miles between his family and Ann Arbor, Michigan.

Regardless, Brady kept working hard and returned to wear the blue and maize gold for the 1998 season. The good news was that he was able to win the starting job over the incoming freshman, Drew Henson. When the decision was announced by Coach Carr in a press release from the school, he stated that Brady had paid his dues as a backup in the program while also showing to the coaching staff that he had an excellent arm and had earned respect from them and his fellow teammates.[xiii]

Brady was able to set school records for the most pass attempts (350) and completions (214) for a completion percentage of 61 percent. Brady did accumulate 2,636 yards and 15 touchdowns, but he also threw 12 interceptions. He also earned an honorable mention on the season's All-Big Ten team and then went on to defeat the Arkansas Razorbacks, who were ranked 11th in the country at that time, in the Florida Citrus Bowl, 45-31, played on January 1, 1999. It was a game where Brady showed his true determination as he led the offense to a 21-point rally in less than five minutes to get the win.[xiv] Brady completed 14 out of 27 of his passes for a total of 209 yards with a 21-yard touchdown pass to wide receiver Diallo Johnson that would give Michigan the lead for good. Despite the game-winning throw, the Citrus Bowl MVP award went to running back Anthony Thomas for having 132 yards and three touchdowns on just 21 rushing attempts in the game.

Henson gained some playing time and showed moments of promise with 21 of 47 passing for 254 yards, three touchdowns, and only interception scattered through seven of Michigan's 13 games, including the Citrus Bowl win. It created some quarterback controversy because of Brady's double-digit number in the statistic line's interception column – a big part of why Coach Carr decided to split time between Brady and Henson in the 1999 season, which was Brady's final year of eligibility.

In his last year of collegiate eligibility, Brady watched Henson start the first quarter of games before he took the ball in the second quarter – the one with the better frame of play which would lead the Wolverine offense in the second half. Despite being a controversial game plan among many Michigan fans and even many in the locker room, Carr was worried that if not given enough playing time, Henson would leave the program since he was receiving plenty of interest to play professional baseball. Yankees owner George Steinbrenner, who just happened to be a fan of Michigan's biggest rival in Ohio State, was ready to offer a three million dollar contract to leave Ann Arbor and join the New York Yankees. Eventually, he would enter the Yankees farm system, but only accumulated a .111 batting average in limited major league action a few years later.

During the span of the dual-quarterback system during the 1999 season, the Wolverines won their first five games, including a 26-22 win over long-time rival Notre Dame at home. Michigan's non-conference schedule also included Rice (37-3) and Syracuse (18-13) before they opened up their conference schedule with a 21-16 win against the Wisconsin Badgers and a 38-12 victory against the Purdue Boilermakers.

It seemed like the system was working for the Wolverines until they lost back to back conference games – a 34-31 defeat to in-state rival Michigan State in East Lansing. Brady had 30 completions out of 40 attempts for 285 yards and two touchdowns while Henson was 6-for-12 for 111 yards, one touchdown, and one interception. The final straw for Carr's plan to split time between both quarterbacks was broken after a 35-29 upset loss at home to the Illinois Fighting Illini where Henson struggled with only two completions while Brady went 23-for-38 for 307 yards, two touchdowns, and two interceptions. The back-to-back losses, including a dropped game to the Illini in front of more than 100,000 fans at their home stadium, affectionately titled "The Big House," led to the change which made Brady the full-time quarterback. Such change was okay for Henson, who years later told Stephen J. Nesbitt of the Michigan Daily that he was fine with Brady taking over full control of the Wolverine offense in November. Important games were coming up in the Big Ten and there had to be consistency for any chance of winning the Big Ten championship[xv]. Besides, Henson acknowledged that he knew his year was coming after Brady graduated. Henson's split time with Brady allowed the former to finish with 47 completions out of 90 attempts for 546 yards, three touchdowns, and two interceptions.

Brady would make the most of his opportunity to be a full-time starter with a run of Big Ten Conference wins against the Indiana Hoosiers, 34-31, on October 30, 1999, and against the Northwestern Wildcats, 37-3, on November 6, 1999. But the final two games of the regular season would be considered two of Brady's best three games wearing the maize gold and blue uniform with the Wolverines.

On November 13, 1999, Brady had some late-game heroics with an 11-yard pass to Marcus Knight with under two minutes left to give the Wolverines a big 31-27 win on the road against the Penn State Nittany Lions – who were nearing the top five in the nation as the sixth-ranked team in the polls – at Beaver Stadium in State College, Pennsylvania[xvi]. While only having 17 completions out of his 36 throws, Brady still had 256 yards to go beyond 2,000 passing yards on the season to be just the second quarterback in school history to accomplish that feat in two consecutive seasons. The first was Todd Collins in 1993 and 1994. It was a big win for the Wolverines as they were about to go back home for their biggest game of the season against the Ohio State Buckeyes.

On November 20, 1999, at Michigan Stadium in Ann Arbor, more than 100,000 fans were about to witness what many have since considered one of the best games in the Michigan-Ohio State rivalry that now features more than 110 total meetings. It was a tough game overall for Brady, who was 17 out of 26 from the field for 150 yards, but he had both of his touchdown passes in the last 16 minutes of the game as the Wolverines earned the 24-17 win over the Buckeyes.[xvii] Down in the second half, 17-10, Brady tied the game up with an eight-yard touchdown pass to Shawn Thompson near the end of the third quarter. But with about five minutes left in the game, Brady would complete a 10-yard touchdown to Marquise Walker to complete the comeback win for Michigan.

By this time, the Wolverines were entering the top 10 in the nation, which they started the season in that part of the national rankings with a peak of being the third best team in the country before a drop sent them all the way down to 16th in the nation in early November. But the Wolverines were finding themselves with a chance to end the season on a high note during New Year's Day 2000 in the annual Orange Bowl played in Miami, Florida. Brady set Michigan and Orange Bowl records after he completed 34 passes out of 46 attempts for 369 yards and four touchdowns in a 35-34 overtime victory against the Alabama Crimson Tide on January 1, 2000.[xviii] In college, both teams would receive a possession starting on the opponent's 25-yard line, and Brady would cover that entire length in one pass to Shawn Thompson for the winning score; Alabama scored a touchdown on their drive but missed the point-after kick to give Michigan the win. Ten of Brady's completions went to wide receiver David Terrell for 150 yards and three touchdowns, who would take the Most Valuable Player honors in a performance that helped Terrell build his stock to become a first-round pick in the 2001 NFL Draft to the Chicago Bears.

The Wolverines also had a talented rushing attack led by Anthony Thomas running for 1,257 yards and 16 touchdowns in 1999 season. But Brady had a much better statistical line than the year before – completing about 61 percent for 2,217 yards, 16 touchdowns, and only six interceptions. With improved throwing strength and accuracy, Brady made a choice to pursue a professional career after earning a Bachelor's Degree in General Studies – focusing on business and psychology. He also had a resume built up just in case, one that he found years later and posted on his Facebook page as a Throwback Thursday post.[xix] Brady earned a grade point average of 3.3 out of 4.0 and had completed an internship at Merrill Lynch in Ann Arbor as an assistant to a senior sales broker for the summers of 1998 and 1999. He listed on his resume that he learned about upper management and company strategy while gaining experience working on stock and mutual fund reports as well as working with client portfolios. He also spent two summers working as a sales representative for the University of Michigan Golf Course and the Polo Fields Golf and Country Club in nearby Jackson. His work experiences also included supervising and managing construction and security for the Top of the Park Summer Festival in Ann Arbor.

Incidentally, at the bottom of the resume, Brady listed his football accomplishments, including his share of the 1997 college football

National Championship and being the team captain and MVP in the 1999 season. Eventually, Brady would enter the NFL Draft, but some were not sure how his career would play out, which was nothing new for Brady since no one expected he was going to leave Ann Arbor with a 20-5 record and two New Year's Day bowl victories.

Still, it's always good to have a backup plan to keep in mind when things look bleak, and Brady had that during the early part of his career in the National Football League.

Chapter 3: Tom's Early Career in the NFL[xx]

Brady entered the 2000 NFL Draft and was somewhat ignored by teams early on and fell to the sixth round where he was the 199th overall pick by the New England Patriots. It was a surprise for some football writers because they felt that his performance in the 2000 Orange Bowl would have built his stock up to be among the early-round selections.

In fact, quarterbacks did not go until the 18th pick when Chad Pennington of Marshall went to the New York Jets. Other quarterbacks that went ahead of Brady included third round selections Giovanni Carmazzi (Hofstra) in the third round to San Francisco, Chris Redman (Louisville) to Baltimore, and fellow sixth-round draft picks Marc Bulger to New Orleans, and Spergon Wynn to Cleveland. It was a much different draft than the previous where when three quarterbacks were selected first, second and third in the 1999 NFL Draft – Tim Couch to Cleveland, Donovan McNabb to Philadelphia and Akili Smith to Cincinnati.[xxi]

Little did anyone know that Brady, going just before Louisiana Tech's Tim Rattay and Jarious Jackson of Notre Dame, was going to have the best career of them all, and it helped that he was going to learn under Drew Bledsoe. Bledsoe was a legend in his right at the time who finished a 14-year career with a total of 44,611 yards and 251 touchdowns.

One of Bledsoe's best seasons was in 1996 season where he completed just fewer than 60 percent of his passes for 4,086 yards and 27 touchdowns against 15 interceptions for an 11-5 record, winning the American Football Conference Championship with a 20-6 win over the Jacksonville Jaguars. The season ended with a loss, however, to the Green Bay Packers 35-21 in Brett Favre's lone Vince Lombardi Trophy.

There were a few playoff appearances for the Patriots since then, but during Brady's rookie year, there were struggles in a 5-11 record and a last-place finish in the AFC East Division. Bledsoe was the starting quarterback with 3,291 yards, 17 touchdowns, and 13 interceptions with a completion rate of 58.8 percent. Brady only saw action in one game on November 23, 2000, in a 34-9 loss on Thanksgiving against the Detroit Lions. Brady had one completion out of three pass attempts for only six yards[xxii]. It was a game where Brady played garbage time in the fourth quarter after Bledsoe completed 17 passes for only 148 yards and two interceptions. The reason Brady did not get a lot of time to start was that he was fourth on the depth chart as John Friesz was the primary backup, followed by Michael Bishop.

The good news was that Brady was going to see a lot more time on the field in his sophomore season with the Patriots – just not as much as anyone would have expected during the preseason. The team looked like they had improved with Bledsoe starting in the first game of the season with 241 yards and two touchdowns during a close 23-17 loss on September 9, 2001. The terrorist attacks on September 11, 2011, delayed the NFL's official Week 2, as well as New England's second game of the 2001 season against the New York Jets. But then Bledsoe was hit hard by linebacker Mo Lewis, which resulted in a sheared blood vessel inside his chest after a tough outing with 18-for-28 completions for 159 yards and two touchdowns[xxiii]. Head coach Bill Belichick attempted to keep Bledsoe in the game in the next series, but it likely only caused his ribs to hurt even more. Brady entered the game with about 2:16 left in regulation and had five completions for 46 yards and a run for nine yards despite not being one of the fastest quarterbacks in the league (he never really had to be in his career). The Patriots fell to 0-2 after the 10-3 loss at home. Brady did have two attempts towards the endzone but was unable to connect with the New England receivers on the final two plays of the game.

The Patriots had a much better result in Brady's first NFL start. New England blew out the Indianapolis Colts 44-13 at Foxboro Stadium on September 30, 2001, although Brady did not have to do much as he went 13-for-23 and 168 yards. Brady's numbers were still better than the Colts' Peyton Manning who threw three interceptions. Two of them were returned for touchdowns by the Patriots defense – a 78-yard return by Otis Smith and a 23-yard return by Ty Law. The Patriots also had a big game running the ball, led by Antowain

25

Smith's 94 yards and two touchdowns. It was the first of several meetings between Brady and Manning, and the first of many times that Brady and the Patriots would defeat Manning and his Colts over the next several NFL seasons.

New England did not want to put too much pressure on Brady, who was gaining experience with Bledsoe out. That was evident in their 30-10 loss to the Miami Dolphins on October 7, 2001, a game where Brady completed 12 out of 24 passes for 86 yards in an offense that struggled to finish with 149 total yards and three fumbles. One of those fumbles was recovered in New England's endzone by Miami defensive end Jason Taylor at the end of the third quarter.

Signs were pointing to a challenging season for the New England Patriots, who were missing their starting quarterback, who was being covered by a young, inexperienced, second-year player who was a sixth-round selection in the draft with a 1-3 start. However, the turning point of the season came from a 29-26 overtime victory at home against the San Diego Chargers on October 14, 2001.

In a game against Doug Flutie – known for his late game heroics while playing for Boston College in the 1984 Orange Bowl for the infamous "Hail Mary" – Brady had completed 33 passes out of 54 for 364 yards and two touchdowns. The first came on a 21-yard pass to Terry Glenn, who finished with seven receptions and 110 yards. The game became a highlight of the season when Brady led a 60-yard-drive in the final two minutes to send the game into overtime with a

26-yard pass to David Patten that set up a short three-yard touchdown toss to Jermaine Wiggins. Brady would go a perfect three-for-three in passing to set up Adam Vinatieri's 44-yard field goal for the win, which started a historic run towards the AFC playoffs.

Brady and the Patriots offense continued to shine with another win over the Indianapolis Colts on October 21, 2001, where he completed 16 of 20 passes for 202 yards and three touchdowns – David Patten had two of them as he finished the game with 117 yards – as New England defeated earned a 38-17 win. Those two games showed that Brady had some potential. But because he was still a young quarterback building experience in the NFL, Brady still had some struggles as a full-time starter in 2001. During a 31-20 loss at Denver on October 28, 2001, Brady threw four interceptions, which included one being returned 39 yards for a pick-six by Denver's Denard Walker near the end of the fourth quarter. Still, Brady finished the game with 203 yards and two touchdowns in the game, but the Patriots were 3-3 at the time of the loss in Denver. Not a bad spot considering that they were being led by the second string quarterback. However, Brady was about to make a charge in the second part of the NFL season that began the Brady legacy.

The Patriots would win eight of their last nine games and would finish the season with a record of 11-5, as well as winning the AFC East Division. During the second-half run, Brady had one of his better games on the road against the Atlanta Falcons on November 4, 2001, where he completed 21 out of 31 passes for 250 yards and three touchdowns in a 24-10 win – Brady had a deep 44-yard touchdown pass to Troy Brown late in the third quarter. A few weeks later on November 25, 2001, Brady threw four touchdown passes in a game for the first time during a 34-17 win over the New Orleans Saints, part of a 19-for-26 for 258 yards that featured a 41-yard touchdown pass to running back Antowain Smith, who also had 111 yards rushing.

It was a successful regular season for Brady, who went 11-3 as a starting quarterback and finished the season with 2,843 passing yards with a completion rate just below 64 percent. He had 18 touchdown passes against 12 interceptions. The 11-5 record also gave them a first round bye that led to hosting the team's first playoff game since the 1998 season. The Patriots would defeat the Oakland Raiders in the AFC Divisional Round on January 19, 2002.

It was a game both known as the "Snow Bowl" and the "Tuck Rule Game." It was a difficult game for both teams as several inches of snow fell onto the field at Foxboro Stadium throughout the match, but the turning point was during the Patriots' final drive with 2:06 left and started at their 46-yard-line with Oakland on top 13-10. After a pass to Kevin Faulk and a run of his own to enter the Raiders side of the field, Brady was sacked by Oakland safety Charles Woodson and caused what appeared to be a game-clinching fumble in which the Raiders were able to recover. However, the play was reviewed by officials in a booth upstairs. The ruling was overturned after it was decided that Brady's arm was coming forward when he was initially hit, and the play was considered an incomplete pass rather than a fumble.

On the very next play, Brady completed a 13-yard pass to Patten that helped set up the game-tying 45-yard field goal by Vinatieri. In overtime, the Patriots were able to drive 61 yards to set up Vinatieri's 23-yard kick for the 16-13 win. Brady completed all eight of his passes on the game-winning drive. However, the controversial call led to the NFL eliminating what was affectionately titled the "tuck rule" more than a decade later in 2013.

Despite the controversy, the Patriots kept the momentum as an underdog team, earning yet another improbable result in their 24-17 win against the Pittsburgh Steelers in the AFC Championship game on January 27, 2002. Brady looked to be on fire with 12-for-18 passing for 115 yards but had to leave the game in the second quarter due to an injured ankle. In entered Bledsoe in his first action since the Week Two injury four months ago, and he was able to complete an 11-yard touchdown pass to Patten to give New England a 14-3 lead moments after Brady's exit. Although Bledsoe had some struggles with 10 completions on 21 passes for 101 yards, it was enough. They had earned their place in Super Bowl XXXVI in what seemed like a fairy tale storyline for Bledsoe. Even though the quarterback who played in the previous Super Bowl appearance had watched from the sideline for several weeks despite being cleared to play weeks after the chest injury he suffered against the Jets in September.

However, the Patriots went back to Brady, the quarterback who led their season to the playoffs, and found themselves matched up against the St. Louis Rams. The Rams were 14-2 in the regular season and led by quarterback Kurt Warner, who had nearly 5,000 yards and 36 touchdowns with weapons like wide receivers Torry Holt and Isaac Bruce and running back Marshall Faulk to compose what many called "the Greatest Show on Turf." With all of those things in mind, the Rams were considered the 14-point favorites to win Super Bowl XXXVI at the Louisiana Superdome in New Orleans, Louisiana.[xxiv]

While the Rams topped the Patriots in offensive numbers with 427 total yards against New England's 267, St. Louis had three turnovers, including one fumble and two interceptions thrown by Warner – one was returned by Law for a 47-yard defensive touchdown for the Patriots. On the other side, Brady went 16-for-27 for 145 yards with one touchdown that came on an 8-yard pass to Patten that gave New England a 14-3 lead and was later extended to 17-3 on Vinatieri's 37-yard field goal in the last third quarter.

Warner, however, would have a 2-yard run and 26-yard pass in the fourth quarter for the Rams to tie the game at 17-17 with less than two minutes left in the match. This gave Brady – who was still only in his first season of being a starting quarterback – less than 1:30 left in regulation. His answer was five-for-seven completions for five, eight, 11, 23, and six yards that set up a 48-yard kick from Vinatieri in the final seconds for the 20-17 upset win for Brady's first NFL championship. It was a dream season for almost the entire Patriots organization and the first for head coach Bill Belichick. But not for Bledsoe, who felt the way Brady debuted in the NFL was not under the best circumstances. In fact, he was eventually traded to the Buffalo Bills in 2002 and had one of the best seasons of his career with 4,359 yards, 24 touchdowns, and 15 interceptions – returning to the Pro Bowl for the fourth time in his career. He would finish his career with two more years with the Bills and two with the Dallas Cowboys.

Brady would have a better year statistically in the 2002 season with 3,764 yards in his first year, starting all 16 games and throwing for 28 touchdowns against 14 interceptions. In the first game of the season, Brady went 29 of 43 for 294 yards and three touchdowns during a 30-14 win at home against the Pittsburgh Steelers on September 9, 2002. A couple of weeks later, Brady set a career high mark with 410 yards and completed 72.2 percent of his 53 total passes during a 41-38 shootout against the Kansas City Chiefs on September 22, 2002. Brady again led a game-winning drive with four out of five passes completed for 46 yards on the opening drive of overtime to allow the veteran Vinatieri to kick the deciding 35-yard field goal.

Overall, Brady showed signs of how good he could be, and he was still a young player at the time with some development still taking place, but the Patriots finished 9-7, which was good enough for second place in the AFC East but not for the playoffs. It might have been many factors that included Brady's continued development and maybe some hangover from winning the Super Bowl. But this championship win over the Rams was just the beginning of what has been one of the greatest careers in NFL history; a quarterback who was still just a sixth-round selection with no expectations coming out of the University of Michigan.

Chapter 4: A Brady Dynasty[xxv]

2003 Season

After missing the playoffs in 2002, the Patriots were able to finish with a 14-2 record to finish first in the AFC East Division in the 2003 season. There were some early bumps in the road as the Patriots lost 31-0 in the first week to the Buffalo Bills on September 7, 2003. In a game where Drew Bledsoe had a chance to host his former backup, he played a lot better with 230 yards and one touchdown while Brady struggled with only 123 yards and four interceptions. One of them was returned 37 yards by Buffalo's Sam Adams for a touchdown in the second quarter of the game. The season-opening loss was quickly followed up by a 31-10 win in Philadelphia on September 14, 2003, where Brady completed 30 out of 44 passes for 255 yards and three touchdowns. But Brady struggled in the next two games with 181 yards in a 23-16 win over the New York Jets on September 21, 2003, and then throwing three interceptions in a 20-17 loss at Washington on September 28, 2003. But Brady would begin to find his groove as the Patriots won 12 games in a row to round out the regular season, throwing only five interceptions during that winning streak and throwing 18 touchdowns and beginning to look like the Kurt Warner, who he faced a few years prior during his first Super Bowl season.

One of Brady's highlight games was on November 3, 2003, on the road against the Denver Broncos where he went 20 for 35 for 350 yards and three touchdowns to give the Patriots a 30-26 win. After giving up a safety to the Broncos defense with 2:49 left in the game for Denver's 26-23 lead, the Patriots defense held the Broncos to go three-and-out to allow Brady to have the ball with 2:15 left. Brady made some big throws that included a 19-yard pass to running back Kevin Faulk to get into Denver territory. Brady completed another pass to Faulk for 16 yards before throwing to David Givens for an 18-yard touchdown to take the 30-26 lead. An interception of Danny Kanell by New England's Asante Samuel sealed the win for New England.

Brady also had 368 yards in a 23-20 win over the Houston Texans on November 23, 2003, where he was going drive for drive with the Texans. Tony Banks led two touchdown drives despite completing only 10 out of 25 throws for only 93 yards. But Brady led another late drive to tie the game at 20-20 after a four-yard touchdown pass to Daniel Graham that concluded an 80-yard drive that lasted about 2:20 with Brady completing five of eight for 74 yards. Both teams had multiple drives before Vinatieri kicked the game-winning 28-yard field goals; another example that Brady knew how to come from behind and help his team win the close games when it mattered. At the same time, Brady would still show in other games that he could be dominant like he was during a 31-0 win on December 27, 2003, against the Buffalo Bills – where Brady exacted some revenge from the season-opening loss in New York. At Gillette Stadium in Foxboro, Massachusetts, Brady had four touchdowns in the first half with a one-yard pass to Daniel Graham on the opening drive and a nine-yard pass to Bethel Johnson moments later. He then had a 19-yard pass within the first minute of the second quarter and then a 10-yard pass to Givens near the end of the first half – highlighting his 204 yards on 21 completed passes.

The way the Patriots ended the season was a complete polar opposite from that 31-0 loss at Buffalo to begin the 2003 season that made some New England fans if the team made a mistake letting Bledsoe go and that Brady was a one-hit wonder in the NFL. With the win at home against Buffalo capping a 12-game winning streak to end the regular season, the Patriots were not only the AFC East Division champions, but they were also the number one seed out of the AFC thanks to Brady finishing a season with 3,620 passing yards, 23 touchdowns, and just 12 interceptions. But the Patriots also had a running game that featured Antowain Smith and Kevin Faulk combining for about 1,200 yards. Faulk was a favorite target for Brady to be a receiver out of the backfield with 440 yards on 48 receptions as well.

After having earned a bye week in the first round of the playoffs, the Patriots defeated the Tennessee Titans in the AFC Divisional Round 17-14 on January 10, 2004, where Brady had some struggles with 21-

of-41 passing for 210 yards and one touchdown. The teams were tied in the fourth quarter until Brady got the Patriots close enough for Vinatieri to nail a 46-yard field goal that would be the go-ahead score.

Still, he played one of his best games against the Indianapolis Colts 24-14 on January 18. As per the usual, Brady defeated Peyton Manning with 22-for-37 for 237 yards and one touchdown – Manning had the same number of yards but allowed four interceptions. However, Vinatieri was once again a star for the team with field goals of 31, 25, 27, 21, and 34 yards. Brady would move the team into position to have the field goal opportunities at least to help the Patriots make a move to compete for the NFL's championship.

Brady would have a much better quarterback matchup when the Patriots faced the Carolina Panthers in Super Bowl XXXVIII on February 1, 2004, at Houston's Reliant Stadium. The Panthers were an 11-5 team in the regular season that was looking for a similar upset the Patriots gained a few years ago in a similar situation against the St. Louis Rams – a team that was entering the game as an underdog. In fact, the Panthers were within that first ten years of their NFL existence and were 1-15 during the 2001 season.[xxvi] Thanks to head coach John Fox, Carolina would improve to 7-9 in 2002 and then to the 11-5 record in 2003. The Panthers were led by a rushing attack with Stephen Davis' 1,444 yards and eight touchdowns while quarterback Jake Delhomme had 3,219 yards, 19 touchdowns, and 16 interceptions.

It did not look like it would be as exciting of a game, but fans filling up Reliant Stadium and the millions watching at home would enjoy one of the most memorable Super Bowl games in NFL history[xxvii]. This was despite not having the controversial halftime performance with Justin Timberlake and Janet Jackson with the infamous wardrobe malfunction.

After a scoreless start from both teams in the first quarter, the Patriots offense got started with Brady striking first with a five-yard touchdown pass to Deion Branch, his favorite target that season, to take the 7-0 lead with only three minutes left in the first half. But Carolina quickly followed up about two minutes later when their quarterback Delhomme completed a 39-yard pass to Steve Smith to tie the game up. The Patriots would have a response as Brady completed a deep 52-yard pass to Branch to set up another short five-yard touchdown throw to David Givens with only 23 seconds left in the half. New England would have a short kickoff that was returned to Carolina's 47-yard-line with 12 seconds left in the half. Carolina's Davis ran 21 yards to help set up a 50-yard field goal by John Kasay before halftime – now there was a game.

Both teams exchanged defensive stances through the third quarter, similar to the slow start in the first quarter. After a two-yard touchdown run by New England's Smith for a 21-10 lead, the Panthers would answer with their rushing touchdown from DeShaun Foster for 33 yards. Later in the quarter, the Delhomme threw a deep pass to top receiver Muhsin Muhammad for an 85-yard touchdown with 6:53 left in the game and a slim 22-21 lead. The Patriots would answer with a long drive starting on their 32-yard-line and finished up with Brady's 1-yard touchdown toss to linebacker Mike Vrabel who entered the game as a tight end.

Still, Delhomme and the Panthers would tie the game at 29-29 with an 80-yard drive that ended in just a little more than a minute after a 12-yard throw to Rick Proehl. But if there is one thing fans had learned about the young Brady at that point, it was that he knew how to put together a drive late in the fourth quarter. With 1:08 left in the game, Brady went four-for-five passing in the final moments for 47 yards through the air to give kicker Adam Vinatieri – the hero of Super Bowl XXXVI – the opportunity to win the game with a 41-yard field goal.

While Vinatieri made the biggest play that won the championship, it was a great game from both quarterbacks, with Brady finishing the game with 32-of-48 passing for 354 yards, three touchdowns, and one interception in an effort that gave him and the Patriots two Vince Lombardi Trophies in three seasons. Carolina's Delhomme was 16-for-33 with 323 yards and three touchdowns with his yards coming on big plays like the 85-yard scoring pass to Muhammad. In addition to winning the Super Bowl, Brady also received the Super Bowl's Most Valuable Player Award.

2004 Season

The Patriots followed that up with a great 14-2 regular season record in 2004 for another AFC East Division Championship and another playoff run. The Patriots would start the season winning the first six games, including a 27-24 win over the Colts where Brady threw for 335 yards with three touchdowns and an interception to open the season on September 9, 2004. A few weeks later, Brady would once again top his former mentor Bledsoe when New England defeated Buffalo 31-17. Brady's 298 yards and two touchdowns beat Bledsoe's 247 and one touchdown against an interception.

Even though Brady put up big numbers week in and week out, there were still games where he did show that he was human. During a home game against the Miami Dolphins on October 10, 2004, Brady had only seven completions for 76 yards. However, he did have two touchdown drives that ended with a 1-yard pass to Graham in the first quarter and a five-yard pass to Givens just before halftime. It was not a pretty game for Brady when looking at the statistics, but it continued a winning streak that the Patriots started the season with. The first loss of the season came on the road against the Pittsburgh Steelers 34-20 on October 31 – a game where Brady had two touchdowns and two interceptions through his 271 yards, but he was the only offense where the Patriots only had five yards on six total rushing attempts. The Patriots would then go on another winning streak of another six games, which included a 315-yard passing game for Brady on

November 22, 2004, against the Kansas City Chiefs with one touchdown to earn the 27-19 win.

It was a game that showed the running game beginning to improve with tailback Corey Dillon's two touchdowns for 98 yards. Dillon also had a 100-yard game with two touchdowns, along with 87 yards and one touchdown from Kevin Faulk in a 42-15 win December 5, 2004, against the Cleveland Browns where the team showed they could still win even when Brady was not playing his best. Brady only threw for 157 yards with one touchdown and one interception while completing only 11 of 20 attempts.

The only other loss of the regular season for New England was December 20, 2004, during a road trip to Miami. Brady had led a long touchdown drive that ended with a two-yard pass to Graham to make their lead 28-17 with less than four minutes left in the game. Miami's A.J. Feely led a drive about 68 yards to allow running back Sammy Morris get the one-yard run to bring the deficit to five points, 28-23. The Patriots had the ball before Brady threw an interception right after the two-minute warning to linebacker Brendon Ayanbadejo; giving the Dolphins a chance to work with a short field at New England's 21-yard-line with about 1:45 left. It only took about 20 seconds before Feeley completed the 21-yard touchdown pass to Derrius Thompson to get the 29-28 lead. While Brady had built a reputation up until that point for making a comeback, he would throw his fourth interception to Dolphins' defensive back Arturo Freeman, which gave Miami just their third win of the season (they would finish 4-12 and last place in the AFC East).

Despite losing to the last place team in the division, New England won their final two games over the New York Jets (23-7) and the San Francisco 49ers (21-17) for that 14-2 record and AFC East crown. Brady had another big year with nearly 3,700 passing yards with 28 touchdowns and 14 interceptions. New England did not have a receiver with 1,000 yards, but Givens had 874 yards with three touchdowns, and David Patten had 800 yards with seven touchdowns. But one of New England's biggest strengths was that they had a premier running back with Corey Dillon having a career year with 1,635 yards and 12 touchdowns.

That rushing attack helped the Patriots defeat the Colts in the AFC Divisional Round on January 16, 2005, at Foxboro Stadium with 144 yards on the ground for Dillon. While Brady was 18-for-27 for 144 yards and a single touchdown through the air on a 5-yard pass to David Givens, the star quarterback added a rushing touchdown of his own on a 1-yard sneak into the end zone in the fourth quarter to cap off a 20-3 win. While not having to do much, it was once again another win over Peyton Manning for Brady.

The Patriots also gained some revenge against Ben Roethlisberger and the Steelers, who were 15-1 on the regular season for the top overall seed with a 41-27 win on January 23, 2005, in the AFC Championship at Pittsburgh's Heinz Field. Brady was 14-of-21 with

207 yards and two touchdowns while Dillon rushed for 73 yards and one touchdown. Branch, who had one of Brady's touchdown passes, scored on a 23-yard run late in the fourth quarter. But Brady's top play was earlier in the game when he connected with Deion Branch for a 60-yard touchdown in the first quarter.

The win brought Brady and his bunch back to the final game of the season as the Patriots went up against the Philadelphia Eagles in Super Bowl XXXIX on February 6, 2005, at Alltel Stadium in Jacksonville, Florida. While the Patriots were once again the favorites, the stadium was filled with fans. Several were rooting for Eagles quarterback Donavan McNabb to grab the brass ring as he was unable to capture the NFC Championship in three attempts in 2001 (28-24 loss to St. Louis), 2002 (27-10 loss to Tampa Bay), and 2003 (14-3 loss to Carolina).

Brady exchanged touchdown passes with McNabb through a 14-14 tie into the fourth quarter, including a 4-yard pass to Givens and a 2-yard pass to Vrabel on a similar play for the linebacker from the previous year's championship game. But the Patriots would jump ahead with a two-yard run from Corey Dillon to jump ahead 21-14, followed by a 22-yard field goal from Vinatieri to extend the lead to 10 points. Still, the Eagles would not go away in what would be McNabb's lone Super Bowl appearance. He was able to lead a 79-yard drive that ended with a 30-yard touchdown pass to Greg Lewis to cut the lead to a single field goal.

Philadelphia attempted an onside kick with 1:47 left in the fourth quarter, but New England would recover and try to run out the clock. The Eagles used all three timeouts while stopping Faulk from getting a first down and forced a punt – giving the McNabb the ball with 46 seconds left. But his lone completion to running back Brian Westbrook was for one yard, and an interception two plays later by safety Rodney Harrison clinched the 24-21 win for the Patriots.

The win gave Brady and Belichick their third Vince Lombardi Trophy in four seasons and was certainly garnering arguments that the Patriots not only had a dynasty but could be an unstoppable force for many years to come. With Brady at the young age of 27, there were questions if he would break the record of most Super Bowl wins among the best quarterbacks of all time. His three wins were already surpassing Broncos legend John Elway (2-3 record in the Super Bowl), Dallas Cowboys' star Roger Staubach (2-2) and Green Bay Packers' quarterback Bart Starr (2-0 and winner of the first two Super Bowls). Despite several great seasons, Brady and the Patriots would not hoist another trophy until the 2014 season – a decade after defeating the Eagles. That did not mean the Patriots struggled as Brady would continue to put up impressive numbers and qualify for the playoffs just about every season. It just turned out that some teams had Brady's number between 2005 and 2014.

Chapter 5: Decade with No Championship

2005 Season

The 2005 NFL season was the first time Brady had reached the 4,000-yard mark for passing yards in a season, completing 63 percent of his passes for 4,110 yards, 26 touchdowns, and 14 interceptions for a quarterback rating of 92.3. Those numbers did not translate into a Super Bowl win like the past two seasons. There were too many severe losses that brought their record down to the 10-6 regular season finish, although it was good enough to earn the crown of the AFC East Division again. The Patriots defense was unable to stop Carolina running back Stephen Davis, who had three touchdowns as the Patriots lost, 27-17, on September 18, 2005. Only a few weeks later, New England suffered an embarrassing loss to the San Diego Chargers at home, 41-17, on October 2, 2005. San Diego had 431 total yards of offense and allowed San Diego's LaDainian Tomlinson have 134 rushing yards and two touchdowns. Despite the struggles, the Patriots were able to accomplish was a 10-6 regular season record for another division title in the AFC East and started off the playoff season with a win in the AFC Wild Card round over the Jacksonville Jaguars 28-3 on January 7, 2006.

But the Patriots would lose in the AFC Divisional Round to Jake Plummer and the Denver Broncos. Despite throwing 20-for-36 for

341 yards and one touchdown, Brady threw two interceptions to a Broncos defense that also held New England's rushing attack to less than 70 yards. Denver would eventually lose to the Pittsburgh Steelers – who then won Super Bowl XL over the Seattle Seahawks. The offseason that followed included the Patriots trying to change their defensive unit with the acquisition of veteran linebacker Junior Seau. But the Patriots also lost some key players before the 2006 season with kicker Adam Vinatieri leaving for the Indianapolis Colts – a departure that would eventually haunt the Patriots down the road.

2006 Season

The Patriots looked to be a strong team in 2006 with a defense that finished the regular season allowing an average of about 14.8 points per game, second in the NFL for that season. The Patriots offense also had two good running backs to help them with the offense, with veteran Corey Dillon rushing for 812 yards and 13 touchdowns, while Laurence Maroney had 745 yards and six touchdowns of his own. This meant that Brady did not have to throw as much and only threw for 3,529 yards, 24 touchdowns, and 12 interceptions in a season that was down statistically from 2005. But the Patriots finished the 2006 regular season with a 12-4 record and another division title, and that success continued in the playoffs, starting with a 37-16 win over the New York Jets during a Wild Card round game on January 7, 2007.

The Patriots would follow up with another win in the AFC Divisional round on January 14, 2007, on the road against the San Diego

Chargers. Brady was able to persevere despite throwing three interceptions and had 280 yards and two touchdowns, including a 4-yard pass to Reche Caldwell to tie the game at 21-21. New England kicker Stephen Gostkowski clinched the win with a 31-yard field goal, maybe showing that the Patriots knew they would be able to find a replacement for the veteran Vinatieri.

However, Brady's long-time rival Peyton Manning, whom he had a history of holding off in the playoffs, would get over the hump that the New England Patriots were for him in the 2006 AFC Championship in Indianapolis. Brady struggled with 232 passing yards with just one touchdown and interception, while Manning had 349 yards and one touchdown to earn a hard fought 38-34 win on January 21, 2007. Manning was able to follow up the rare win over Brady and the Patriots with helping the Colts defeat the Chicago Bears two weeks later – a 29-17 win February 4, 2007, in Super Bowl XLI in Miami. While Manning was not the big reason for the Colts winning the Super Bowl, it was an achievement that Brady had a hand in preventing the Colts star player from enjoying for several years before and after this point in NFL history.

2007 Season

In 2007, the Patriots looked like they were going to be a team of destiny in more ways than one, starting with Brady who would finish the season as the league's Most Valuable Player award with nearly 69 percent of his passes completed for 4,806 yards, 50 touchdowns, and only eight interceptions. His two favorite wide receivers were Randy Moss (1,493 yards and 23 touchdowns) and Wes Welker (1,175 yards and eight touchdowns).

The first week of the season was a good indicator of the type of season Brady would have as he completed 22 out of 28 passes for 297 yards and three touchdowns in a 38-14 win over the New York Jets on September 9, 2007. But the Patriots showed they had an overall team that was going to compete well against the rest of the NFL with the offense totaling 431 yards and a defense that held the Jets to just 227 yards. The special teams unit shined with a 108-yard kickoff return from Ellis Hobbs to start the second half of the season-opening win – a common theme as the Patriots would not see a zero in the loss column throughout the entire regular season.

Brady would continue to have huge games that included 388 yards and five touchdowns at Dallas in a 48-27 win on October 14, 2007 and 373 yards and five touchdowns in a 56-10 win on November 18, 2007 over the Buffalo Bills. He then had 399 yards and four touchdowns against the Pittsburgh Steelers in a 34-13 win on December 9, 2007. Usually, when teams had clinched a first-round bye and the number-one seed's home field advantage throughout the playoffs, teams rested their star players. But the Patriots wanted to claim history as they defeated the New York Giants 38-35 on December 29, 2007. Brady played the entire game with 356 yards and two touchdowns. Brady had his best game of the season during a 49-28 win against the lowly Miami Dolphins – who finished 1-15 on the season – on October 21, 2007. Brady had deep touchdown passes to Donte' Stallworth for 30 yards in the first quarter, followed by touchdown passes of 35 and 50 yards to Randy Moss in consecutive drives before scoring on a 14-yard pass to Wes Welker before halftime to lead 42-7. Brady would finish the game with only four incompletions, and out of the 21 he did complete, he had 354 yards and six touchdowns with an extremely high quarterback rating of 158.3.

Out of the 16 games in the season, Brady had ten games where he did not throw any interceptions. There were four games with just one interception and two games where he had more than one – November 4, 2007, in a 24-20 win over the Indianapolis Colts and then again on December 23, 2007, during a 28-7 win over the Miami Dolphins. Brady looked almost unbeatable with a strong Patriots offense and a stingy defense to go along with it. The only game where he went without a touchdown was on December 16, 2007, where Brady had the worst game of his career as a starter with 14 completions out of 27 attempts for 140 yards and an interception. But the Patriots' defense held the Jets to 234 offensive yards for the 20-10 win. Even when Brady struggled, the Patriots would find a way to win handily.

It was the first time any team had finished the 16-game regular season undefeated, with people wondering if this would be the team to break the 17-0 championship season of the 1972 Miami Dolphins. Back then, teams only played 14 games in the regular season before the

Dolphins claimed Super Bowl VII over the Washington Redskins 14-7 on January 14, 1973.

The Patriots would make easy work of their playoff competition in the AFC playoffs, defeating the Jacksonville Jaguars 31-20 on January 12, 2008. Brady looked strong with 26 out of 28 completions for 262 yards and three touchdowns. But Brady did not have a strong game during the AFC Championship on January 20, 2008, against the San Diego Chargers. In fact, he threw three interceptions for just 209 yards. He did have touchdown drives that ended with a 12-yard pass to Jabar Gaffney in the second quarter and then a 6-yard pass in the early part of the fourth quarter to clinch the 21-12 win. San Diego could not get any offense going with their 311 yards; all of their points came from field goals of 26, 23, 40, and 24 yards from Nate Kaeding. This showed that the Patriots defense was able to hold strong and wanted to help make sure they were doing their part in being part of the historic 19-0 season that fans were starting to think was a real possibility.

No one wanted to pick against the Patriots, especially considering that they were playing the Giants again, who had an improbable run by defeating Tampa Bay, 24-14, Dallas Cowboys, 21-17, and the Green Bay Packers, 17-14, all on the road. They barely made the playoffs with a 10-6 record, and there were talks about head coach Tom Coughlin being released from the team.

The underdogs would gain a surprising victory over the Patriots to give them their first loss in Super Bowl XLII on February 3, 2008, at the University of Phoenix Stadium in Glendale, Arizona. Late in the game with less than a minute left, Eli Manning – the younger brother of Peyton Manning – threw a deep pass for 32 yards to David Tyree, who caught the ball with one hand against his helmet in the highlight play. It helped set up the eventual game-winning touchdown pass from Manning to Plaxico Burress for 13 yards and the Vince Lombardi Trophy.

The Patriots only had 274 yards of offense while Brady completed only 29 out of his 48 passes for 266 yards and just one touchdown from a six-yard pass to Moss. But New England's offensive momentum sputtered due in part to the lack of a consistent rushing offense. Maroney led the team with a whopping 36 yards and one touchdown on his 14 carries. It was a game where Brady had to do everything against a Giants defense that carried them through the NFC playoffs for what some fans would call a "giant upset" – the pun was likely intended.

To say the least, it was a heartbreaking loss for Brady and the Patriots. Yet, a bigger loss was suffered at the beginning of the 2008 season that would take the fans by surprise.

2008 Season

Brady played in the first week at home against the Kansas City Chiefs, but after a good start with seven out of 11 passes completed for 76 yards after about eight minutes into the season, he threw a deep pass to Randy Moss down the field – just like he did many times in 2007. Unfortunately, this time around, Kansas City safety Bernard Pollard came in hitting Brady below the knees and brought the three-time Super Bowl champion crumbling to the ground.

While he walked off the field assisted by team doctors, Brady was shut down for the rest of the season. Tests found that he had a torn anterior cruciate ligaments (ACL) and medial collateral ligaments (MCL) in his left knee. Luckily, an MRI done the next day showed no other torn ligaments or cartilage. Doctors waited for the MCL to heal before repairing, with surgeries done one month after the injury took place, and Brady was then put on a recovery plan that lasted several months.

It was a tough season for the Patriots, who had to depend on Matt Cassell to take over, similar to how Brady stepped up when Bledsoe went down – only there would be no playoff berth awaiting the Patriots despite an 11-5 finish. Cassel made early attempts to fit into the Patriots offense and took his lumps similar to how Brady performed in that 2001 season. In his first career NFL start, Cassel completed 16 of 23 passes for 165 yards while being sacked four times in the game. However, the Patriots kicker Stephen Gostkowski had four field goals of 21, 27, 28, and 27 yards to lead the scoring for New England in a 19-10 win on the road against the New York Jets. Cassel would struggle the very next game with 19 of 31 completed for 131 yards and a touchdown in a 38-13 loss at home to Miami.

Cassel would throw for 3,693 yards, 21 touchdowns, and 11 interceptions on the season and would eventually help the Patriots win five of their last six games on the season to finish 11-5, good enough for second place in the AFC East Division. It was a rare sight to see the Patriots not win the division during Brady's career, but it happened in 2002 and 2008. Many New England fans might have considered this to be the lost season that could have been historic, just like any season Brady played in his career. But there is the old saying that there is always next year when it came to Brady returning from his injury. However, unlike Brady stepping up in the 2001 season for the injured Bledsoe, the Patriots were not planning to put Cassel in the starting spot ahead of their veteran quarterback. In fact, the Patriots did not mind allowing Cassel to leave the team as he signed a lucrative contract with the Kansas City Chiefs. His success was questionable moving forward. He has since become a journeyman quarterback found second or third on the depth charts of teams like the Dallas Cowboys and Minnesota Vikings, getting starts here and there. Brady, on the other hand, returned to form to begin the 2009 season with the hope of the Patriots returning to the playoffs, which they did.

2009 Season

With the bad aftertaste left behind from last season, the Brady had to find his groove in the New England offense for the 2009 season. He did complete 73.6 percent of his passes in the season-opener on September 14, 2009, during a 25-24 win over the Buffalo Bills. Brady struggled at first before leading two touchdown drives in the final 2:06 in regulation for the win – both ended with touchdown passes to Ben Watson of 18 and 16 yards. Brady finished with 378 yards in the game and was sacked once for a big loss, but fans were just happy that Brady got up and continued another strong season.

New England started the season with a 3-2 record with some fans wondering if Brady was starting to suffer a decline as a long-term side effect of the 2008 leg injury. But those doubts went away during the Patriots' 59-0 win over the Tennessee Titans on October 18, 2009. Brady completed 29 out of 34 passes (85.3 percent) for 380 yards and six touchdowns – five of which came in the second quarter during the final 10 minutes of the half and Brady's game was done after completing a nine-yard touchdown pass to Moss for the third time in the match.

That did not mean the Patriots did not have their share of struggles with some losses in the schedule that took some fans by surprise, like a 22-21 loss on December 6, 2009, where Brady had 19 of 29 passes for 352 yards, two touchdowns, and two untimely interceptions. Near the end of the season, the Patriots struggled with some inefficient games including the 115 yards after completing 47.8 percent of his throws in a 17-10 win over the Buffalo Bills on December 20, 2009. Brady also finished the regular season on a sour note as he had only 186 yards and an interception in a 34-27 loss to the Houston Texans.

The Patriots finished 10-6 and first in the AFC East Division. Brady finished with another 4,000+ yard season with 4,398 yards, 28 touchdowns, and 13 interceptions for a 96.2 rating. Considering the injury from the previous season, Brady would win the NFL Comeback Player of the Year award, which should not have come as any surprise to anyone within or watching the NFL that year. Fans were happy to have their quarterback starting again and winning the division championship to earn their regular place in the playoffs. Even if they were able to hold off the New York Jets for that automatic berth in the playoffs and would have likely missed the playoffs without it when considering that had the Patriots lost one more game, they would have entered a four-way tie with Baltimore Ravens, Pittsburgh Steelers, and Houston Texans where they might not have had any tiebreaker advantages to earning either of the two wild-card playoff spots in the conference. While fans were happy just to make the playoffs, this was not the championship contending team that regularly looked like favorites to go to the Super Bowl year in and year out like the dynasty Brady led between 2001 and 2004.

However, the Patriots were upset in the AFC Wild Card Round by the Baltimore Ravens in a 33-14 loss on January 10, 2010, where Brady had one of his worst games in his playoff career with only 154 yards with two touchdowns, three interceptions, and one lost fumble on the team's first drive. The Ravens looked like a strong team that barely made the playoffs after they jumped ahead with a 24-point first quarter that was the big difference in the game. The Patriots outscored the Ravens 14-9 in the second, third and fourth quarters. New England's defense struggled against the run as Ravens running back Ray Rice had 159 yards with two touchdowns that included an 83-yard run during the first play from scrimmage in the first quarter.

2010 Season

New England would return not intending to barely make the playoffs by winning the AFC East. They wanted to restore the dominance that Patriots were known for in the NFL. It started off well. Brady would have 258 yards and three touchdowns during a season-opening win over the Cincinnati Bengals, 38-24, on September 12, 2010. But a loss visiting the Jets, 28-14, the next week where Brady had two interceptions brought some fans to worry about the team's future. Was Brady able to handle being the star player the franchise could depend on after the horrific 2008 injury? By the end of the regular season, the answer was an emphatic yes.

Brady never threw for a lot of yards in most of New England's winning ways where they went 13-1 after the loss to the Jets. But the offense still scored a lot of points to lead the NFL with 518 points (an average of about 32.4 points per game in 2010). Brady still had some good games, but the offense did not have to rely solely on their quarterback as running back BenJarvus Green-Ellis had 1,008 yards and 13 touchdowns along with another 547 yards and five touchdowns from Danny Woodhead. But Brady had one of his best seasons concerning turnovers, throwing only four interceptions on the season – two in the early season loss to the Jets and then another two in the 23-20 win over the Baltimore Ravens on October 17, 2010.

Brady had his best string of games after the 34-14 loss to the Cleveland Browns on November 11, 2007. Brady would throw for 350 yards and three touchdowns in the 39-26 win over the Pittsburgh Steelers, which was followed by completing 76 percent of his passes during a 31-28 win over the Indianapolis Colts on November 21, 2010. Brady only had to complete 19 of 25 for 181 yards and two touchdowns while Green-Ellis and Woodhead combined for 165 yards and two touchdowns. Brady would then have back-to-back games where he had four touchdowns in each of those weeks. It started with the Patriots' 45-24 win over the Detroit Lions on Thanksgiving on November 25, 2010, where he completed 21 out of 27 passes for 341 yards. This was followed up with having 326 yards after completing 21 out of 29 passes in a 45-3 win over the Jets at home in Foxboro, Massachusetts.

Brady was not needed much in the final two games except for first half performances that nearly sealed a 34-3 win at Buffalo on December 26, 2010, and then the 38-7 win against the Dolphins on January 2, 2010. At the end of the regular season, the Patriots once again won the AFC East Division crown and also the number one seed overall in the conference with a 14-2 record in the 2010 regular season. New England was led by Brady's 3,900 yards and 36 touchdowns for a QB rating of 111.0 because he only had four interceptions to win the NFL MVP award once again. So many thought that maybe the Patriots were bound for that fifth Super Bowl win for Brady.

Unfortunately, the Patriots were upset in the Divisional Round by division rival New York Jets 28-21 on January 16, 2011. In the two regular season matchups, the Patriots lost at New York 28-14, but won 45-3 at Gillette Stadium. But during the playoff match in New England's stadium, Brady threw 29-for-45 for 299 yards, two touchdowns, and one interception that came during New England's first offensive drive of the game. The opposing quarterback Mark Sanchez was 16-for-25 with 194 yards and three touchdowns. Brady attempted to engineer a comeback that started with a drive and concluded with a 35-yard field goal from Shayne Graham. But the Jets had a quick touchdown drive where Shonn Greene had a 16-yard touchdown with 1:41 left in the game. Brady led the Patriots to complete a one-minute drive that ended with a 13-yard pass to Branch, but the following onside kick was recovered by the Jets to seal the victory. New York would lose to the eventual Super Bowl champion Pittsburgh Steelers, and Patriots fans were once again left with an early exit in the playoffs despite having the best record in the NFL with a lot of promise from the regular season that was never fulfilled.

2011 Season

The 2011 NFL season was a unique one for the Patriots with an offense that was primarily led by Brady. It started in the first game of the season on September 12, 2011, where he completed 32 out of 48 passes for 517 yards and four touchdowns during a 38-24 win over the Dolphins in Miami. One week later on September 18, 2011, Brady had another 423 yards after completing 31 out of 40 of his throws for three touchdowns during a 35-21 win at home against the San Diego Chargers.

There was one game where Brady had four interceptions in a competitive 34-31 loss at Buffalo on September 25, 2011, where he also had a decent game with 30 of 45 passes for 387 yards and four touchdowns. But one of those interceptions thrown by Brady was returned by Buffalo's Drayton Florence for a 27-yard touchdown. Brady almost led a come-from-behind win with a six-yard touchdown pass to Welker with 3:25 left, but the Bills led a drive of their own behind Ryan Fitzpatrick that allowed Rian Lindell to hit a 28-yard field goal. Brady did not let a game like that happen again as he was only going to throw two interceptions in the final eight games that New England had won to end the regular season as one of the hottest teams in the league. Brady had 19 touchdowns to just two interceptions in that winning streak to conclude the season. The Patriots would finish the year with a 13-3 record to once again give them the AFC East and the top overall seed in the conference for the start of the playoffs. It was a successful 13-win season where Brady was the entire offense for New England with 5,235 passing yards, 39 touchdowns, and 12 interceptions. Brady finished with a final 105.6 quarterback rating and was depended on as the primary source of offense because the Patriots were a team with no running back reaching the 700-yard mark in the regular season. Green-Ellis led the team with 667 yards and 11 touchdowns. New England did have 1,764 rushing yards as a team with contributions from Steven Ridley and Danny Woodhead.

Doubts that New England did not have a consistent running back who could help balance the offense did worry some New England fans. But when Brady is on fire, that is all the offense you need. The Patriots won their divisional round game against the Denver Broncos 45-10 on January 14, 2012, behind Brady's 363 yards and six touchdowns. It was a game where Brady could do not a whole lot wrong with the highlight throw coming on a 61-yard pass to Deion Branch late in the second quarter. But the Patriots defense was able to force Denver quarterback to make a lot of bad throws as he finished the game with just nine completions out of 26 attempts for 136 yards. The win put an end to the Tebowmania that had swept the NFL fan base after possibly one of the worst quarterbacks to have a winning record had defeated the Pittsburgh Steelers in the Wild Card with 316 yards on just ten completions.

Next, the Patriots defeated the Baltimore Ravens in a 23-20 decision on January 22, 2012. While Brady struggled with two interceptions and only 239 yards through the air, it was his 1-yard touchdown run in the fourth quarter that made the difference. The New England defense did just enough to hold off a Ravens offense led by quarterback Joe Flacco's 306 yards on 22 completions.

It looked like the Patriots were on their way to another Super Bowl, but just like in the 2007 season, Brady was bested by the younger Manning, Eli, and the New York Giants 21-17 in Super Bowl XLVI on February 5, 2012, at Lucas Oil Stadium. Brady was 27 out of 41 for 276 yards and two touchdowns. New England had a nice 10-9 lead at halftime before Brady led a touchdown drive at the beginning of the third quarter with a 12-yard pass to tight end Aaron Hernandez to give New England the 17-9 lead. After a few field goals in the third quarter by Giants' kicker Lawrence Tynes (38 and 33 yards each), New York was able to complete the 12-point rally with a six-yard touchdown run by Ahmad Bradshaw gave the Giants the 21-17 lead with 57 seconds left in regulation.

Brady attempted to make a comeback drive by slowly inching the Patriots to their 49-yard-line after a 19-yard pass to Branch and an 11-yard pass to Hernandez, followed by a five-yard defensive offside from Justin Tuck set up two more attempts by Brady with nine seconds left. But the Patriots' quarterback was not able to connect deep with either Branch or Hernandez for the game-winning touchdown and allowed the Giants to get their second Super Bowl championship with Eli Manning leading the offense. It was an incredible end for the New York Giants who were 7-7 in December, and it looked like their head coach Tom Coughlin was possibly going to be let go at the end of the season, similar to the 2007 season. Eli was the Super Bowl MVP recipient after he had completed 30 out of

40 passes for 296 yards and the one touchdown that came on a two-yard pass to Victor Cruz in the first quarter of the game.

However, it was a frustrating end for the Patriots because most of the time, the Giants were a mediocre team that would occasionally make the playoffs with some seasons where Eli would have more interceptions than touchdowns. And yet after the Super Bowl XLVI win, Eli Manning had the same number of Super Bowl MVP awards as Brady. It was another frustrating end despite making it to the Super Bowl, this time because the Patriots were the favorites to win and were upset in another "giant" Super Bowl upset.

2012 Season

It is not a secret that Brady has been the leader for the New England offense for several seasons and a lot of the weight was put on his shoulders. That is what a good quarterback in professional football can do, and in 2012, he continued to do that. But he would have help from other sources in the rushing offense.

The Patriots would return to the playoffs with another 12-win season in 2012. Brady would throw for 4,827 yards, 34 touchdowns, and only eight interceptions. One of his better games of the season came on the road during a 45-7 rout of the St. Louis Rams on October 28, 2012, where Brady completed 23 out of 35 throws for 304 yards and four touchdowns. He had another four-touchdown game on December 10, 2012, during a 42-14 win over the Houston Texans. Most of the games Brady played in yielded 300 yards or more, including a season-high 443 yards in a 41-34 loss to the San Francisco 49ers on December 16, 2012, where Brady threw a career-high 65 passes with only 36 completions.

While Brady was once again putting up some big numbers in the passing game, this time there was help from the run game to give the Patriots the number-one ranked scoring offense with a total of 557 points with an average of 34.8 points per game. That is because running back Stevan Ridley finished the season with 1,263 rushing yards and 12 touchdowns in his second season in the NFL. The former LSU Tigers star had just four games with 100 yards or more, but his big highlight came from the October 7, 2012, win over the Denver Broncos, 31-21. He had 28 carries for 151 yards and an eight-yard touchdown run. He put up the yardage to help the Patriots have a balanced offense that escaped them the past few years, which benefitted a veteran quarterback who now had an offense that allowed him to have different options. He did not have to do all of the work himself like before. This allowed him to remain focused, which was reflected in his final interception numbers. However, while the running backs were improving the offense with more balance, they also had some plays in the passing game as well to help the Patriots win the AFC East again, and the second seed in the conference behind the top-seeded Denver Broncos that were led by the newly acquired Peyton Manning.

A perfect example of the running backs acting as targets out of the backfield for Brady could be found during the AFC playoffs where

New England would take care of business in the Divisional Round with a 41-28 win over the Houston Texas on January 13, 2013. It was a game where Brady threw for 344 yards and three touchdowns. Brady had two of those three touchdown passes go to running backs in the game – Shane Vereen had an eight-yard touchdown catch in the second quarter and one for 33 yards in the fourth quarter.

But Joe Flacco would be the season spoiler again for the Patriots as New England fell 28-13 to the Baltimore Ravens in the AFC Championship on January 20, 2013 – in which Brady threw for 320 yards, one touchdown, and two interceptions. New England looked like a strong team at halftime with the 13-7 lead after Brady had a short goal-line touchdown pass to Welker. But the Ravens had a 21-point swing where Flacco completed a five-yard pass to tight end Dennis Pitta, and then two fourth-quarter touchdown passes to Anquan Bolden. In New England's final offensive drives in the fourth quarter, Brady was unable to find his receiver with one interception going to Baltimore's Darnelle Ellerbe with just under seven minutes left in the game. Brady would get the ball with a little more than two minutes left before eventually throwing an interception to Cary Williams to ultimately guarantee the upset win in the AFC Championship.

The Ravens would move on to defeat the San Francisco 49ers and claim the Vince Lombardi Trophy in a memorable game where the Harbaugh brothers were coaching on opposite sides of the field. John

Harbaugh and his Ravens had the win over his brother Jim and his 49ers.

2013 Season

It was beginning to feel like clockwork for the Patriots as they won another 12 games in the 2013 season along with another AFC East Division Championship where Brady had another incredible season statistically – 4,343 yards and 25 touchdowns against 11 interceptions. That did not mean Brady was without struggles early in the season after completing only 55.8 percent of his passes during the 23-21 win over the Buffalo Bills on September 8, 2013. He had 288 yards, two touchdowns, and one interception. Two field goals from Gostkowski in the fourth quarter, which included a 35 yard kick with five seconds left, allowed New England to escape with the road win. Sure, Brady did not have the game-winning touchdown, but he was still showing that he could lead an offensive drive late in the fourth quarter to set up a game-winning field goal regardless of who was kicking for the Patriots.

It would take Brady some time to find a consistent rhythm throwing the ball as there were many games where he completed below 60 percent of his throws. His lowest percentage was on October 6, 2013, where he completed only 18 out of 38 attempts (47.4 percent) for only 197 yards and an interception in an embarrassing 13-6 loss to the Cincinnati Bengals. Brady was pressured often and was sacked four times in the game. Later in the month on October 27, 2013, Brady had just 13 completions for 116 yards, but he completed a 14-yard touchdown pass to Aaron Dobson to start a 24-point offensive rally that gave the Patriots a 27-17 win over the Miami Dolphins. It was quickly followed by a dominant 55-31 win over the Pittsburgh Steelers on November 3, 2013, where Brady had 432 yards and four touchdowns that included an 81-yard pass to Dobson late in the fourth quarter. This showed that Dobson had some promise as an under the radar receiver who could make some players as he collected 519 yards and four touchdowns on the season. Brady has always made a habit of helping wide receivers develop well, just like he did with Welker and Woodhead.

With the division looking more and more in their favor near the end of the regular season. Despite a 24-20 loss in Miami, Brady was able to get some rest in the final two games as the Patriots improved rushing attack was able to lead the way to a 41-7 win over the Baltimore Ravens on December 22, 2013, where LeGarrette Blount led the team with 76 yards and two touchdowns. This was followed up with Blount rushing for 189 yards and two more touchdowns to help the Patriots get the 34-20 win over the Bills on December 29, 2013. Blount had finished the regular season with 772 rushing yards and seven touchdowns to support Stevan Ridley's 773 yards and seven touchdowns.

After enjoying another bye week in the NFL playoffs, the Patriots would move on to defeat the Indianapolis Colts during the AFC Divisional Round. But unlike the time Brady faced a Manning-led

64

Colts, this time they were led by the young star Andrew Luck with a 43-22 victory on January 12, 2014, in a game that was won with the feat of LeGarrette Blount – 166 yards and four touchdowns. Brady did fine with 198 passing yards after completing just 13 out of 25 throws.

Peyton Manning, however, would get the best of Brady for only the second time in several playoff attempts. Manning, no longer the quarterback for the Indianapolis Colts, would succeed with the Denver Broncos and defeated the Patriots 26-16 in the AFC Championship game on January 19, 2014, at Sports Authority Field at Mile High Stadium. While Brady threw for 277 yards and one touchdown, Manning threw for 400 yards and two touchdowns. Brady tried to will his team to a victory by earning a five-yard touchdown run with 3:07 left in the game. But Manning had a 23-yard pass to Jacob Tamme and several key runs from Montee Ball to drain the rest of the clock to give the Broncos the win and send Manning to his third career Super Bowl appearance. It was a short-lived victory, though, as the Broncos walked into the buzz-saw that was the Seattle Seahawks defense in a 43-8 Super Bowl XLVIII defeat on February 2, 2014.

Just like the other nine seasons before the 2013 season, Brady was once again without a Vince Lombardi Trophy in his hand at the end of the season after having won three out of his first four seasons as a starting quarterback in his career. While continuing to establish himself as one of the greatest quarterbacks in NFL history, not winning a Super Bowl in several great seasons was a frustrating trend for himself and the organization. Still, the streak of seasons without winning a Super Bowl would come to an end soon, and it would come as somewhat of a surprise considering who they were going to face in that championship game. But the New England fans were faithful enough in hopes that they would see Brady earn his fourth championship to put himself in the ranks against some of the NFL's all-time greats like Joe Montana and Terry Bradshaw, even if his career statistics already put him up there in the all-time great discussion.

Chapter 6: Breaking the Hump in the 2014 Season

There were some frustrations and hopes for a strong season to finally yield the first Super Bowl championship in 10 years for the New England Patriots and Tom Brady, who was hoping to be only the third quarterback in NFL history to win four Vince Lombardi trophies. Terry Bradshaw won in 1975, 1976, 1979, and 1980 with the Pittsburgh Steelers, while Joe Montana won in 1982, 1985, 1989, and 1990 with the San Francisco 49ers.

He was already tied for the most Super Bowl appearances with John Elway, who was 2-3 overall in the big game with the Denver Broncos and retired after winning back-to-back championships in Super Bowl XXXII (1998) and XXXIII (1999). But older players usually begin to fight against age and the diminishing skills that follow. Brady turned 37 during the 2014 season, and the first week was an early sign proving that such could be the case.

On September 7, 2014, the Patriots fell to the Miami Dolphins – a rival in the AFC East – 33-20 at the Dolphins' Sun Life Stadium. It looked like the Patriots were on their way to an early 1-0 start as Brady completed a red-zone touchdown pass for six yards to tight end Rob Gronkowski en route to a 20-10 halftime lead. But the defense faltered as Miami quarterback threw for two touchdowns, and

Knowshon Moreno ran for 134 yards and a touchdown of his own to give the Patriots a 0-1 start.

Brady had games of lower yardage in the next three games as the Patriots moved to 2-2 on the first part of the season, including a 30-7 win on September 14, 2014, in Minnesota against the Vikings. Brady had only 149 passing yards that included a nine-yard touchdown pass to receiver Julian Edelman. The Patriots' defensive and special team units shined with a 58-yard blocked punt returned by Chandler Jones as New England began to run away with the game just before halftime. The next week on September 21, the Patriots had what many would have thought to be an easy win over the Oakland Raiders, a team that had averaged between three to four wins since the infamous "Tuck Rule Game."

Surprisingly, New England only won 16-9 at home in Gillette Stadium. Brady and Gronkowski were given credit for the game's lone touchdown on a 6-yard pass late in the second quarter. Brady finished 24-of-37 passing for 234 yards, but Patriots' kicker was the star with three field goals for 21, 20, and 36 yards respectively.

The Patriots' struggles on offense would bite them in a road game on September 29th in Kansas City, Montana. New England fell in a 41-14 game against the Chiefs. The Chiefs went on a 27-0 run to start the game thanks to running back Jamaal Charles with one rushing touchdown and two receiving touchdowns from the arm of Alex Smith. While Brady scored one touchdown from a 44-yard pass to

Brandon LaFell to prevent the shutout, he had only 14 completions for 159 yards and two interceptions. His backup, rookie Jimmy Garoppolo from Eastern Illinois University, was six-for-seven for 70 yards and a 13-yard touchdown pass to Gronkowski late in the game.

Granted, there was not going to be a quarterback controversy after one week when comparing the performance of a veteran with three Super Bowl championships and a rookie from a small college football program who had played one quarter. Perhaps it played a part in Brady and the Patriots having an offensive explosion in their next game at home against the Cincinnati Bengals – a 43-17 victory on October 5, 2014. Brady threw for 23-of-35 for 292 yards and two touchdowns and was helped with 113 yards rushing from Stevan Ridley and another 90 for running back Shane Vereen to give New England more than 500 total offensive yards in the first win of a seven-game winning streak.

During that streak, Brady had highlight games that included a 37-22 win over the Buffalo Bills on October 12, 2014, at Ralph Wilson Stadium. He threw for 361 yards and four touchdowns, including a 56-yard deep touchdown to Brandon LaFell to cap off the win.

A few weeks later, the Patriots hosted the Chicago Bears on October 26, 2014, where Brady had a near perfect performance with 30-of-35 passes completed for 354 yards and five touchdowns. Four came in the first half for a 38-7 lead at the break including two touchdowns to Gronkowski, one to Tim Wright and another to LaFell. Brady had his fifth on a 46-yard pass to Gronkowski, who was starting to become one of Brady's favorite targets as a big tight end who could power over a majority of defenders in the league.

Later in the regular season, Brady also gained some revenge against the Miami Dolphins with a blowout 41-13 win at home on December 14, 2014. Brady had 287 yards on 21 completions with two touchdowns. While Dolphins' quarterback Ryan Tannehill had more yards through the air with 346, he also threw two interceptions with not as much help from running back Moreno in the second game against the Patriots.

They then suffered a 17-9 loss to the Bills in the final week of the season on December 28, 2014, a game where most of the starters came off the field with a first round bye week and home field advantage clinched. The Patriots still won the AFC East Division championship – as they have for nearly every season under Brady's command.

The long-time quarterback finished with an efficient season, completing 64 percent of his passes for 4,109 yards and 33 touchdowns while throwing only nine interceptions for a 97.4 quarterback rating. The season would not be a success without reaching and reclaiming the Vince Lombardi Trophy. The first roadblock in the path to Super Bowl XLIX was an AFC Divisional round matchup on January 10, 2015, against Joe Flacco and the

Baltimore Ravens, who had a history of eliminating the Patriots from the playoffs over the past few seasons.

At one point, it looked like the Ravens were going to spoil the season once again as Flacco was 28-for-45 for 292 yards and four touchdowns. However, Brady would throw the game-winning touchdown late in the fourth quarter with a 23-yard pass to LaFell to give the Patriots the 35-31 win. Brady finished the game with 33 completions out of 50 throws for 367 yards and three touchdowns and a 4-yard rushing touchdown in a game where the Patriots had only 14 total yards on the ground.

New England would get much better production in their rushing attack eight days later in a 45-7 win against the Indianapolis Colts, who had gained an upset victory the week before against Peyton Manning and the Denver Broncos. While Brady had 23 completions out of 35 attempts that collected 226 yards with three passing scores, running back LeGarrette Blount had 30 carries for 148 yards and three touchdowns to bring the Patriots back to the Super Bowl stage where Brady had lost the last two times they made it.

In the days that followed the conference championships, the headlines in Boston and much of the country were not focused on how the Patriots defeated the Colts, but rather the question of footballs and the proper air pressure after a few players from Indianapolis complained. A report from NFL insiders later announced that league officials found 11 of the 12 balls the Patriots used were under-inflated by two pounds each for the AFC Championship.

In the days that followed, there were more questions about the air pressure of footballs – which the NFL requires to be around two pounds per square inch lower than the NFL minimum of 12.5 psi. As the Patriots were preparing for their return to the Super Bowl, the NFL organized an investigation team led by Ted Wells, an attorney known for leading the investigation of a bullying scandal within the Miami Dolphins organization less than two years prior.

However, the results would not be announced until months after the Super Bowl, so the questions of who was behind the deflating of footballs was on hold. The Patriots found themselves against the defending champions from Seattle in Glendale, Arizona. The Seahawks were led by the unique threat of quarterback Russell Wilson, who was a dual-threat passer and runner who made plays along with running back Marshawn Lynch – one of the most consistent power running backs. Both players were able to overcome the high-octane Broncos the year before in a 43-8 blowout win in Super Bowl XLVIII to end the 2013 season.

The game was deadlocked through the first quarter until Brady led a drive that concluded with an 11-yard pass to LaFell for the early 7-0 lead. The Seahawks continued to push their running game and eventually tied the game with a three-yard run into the end-zone with 2:16 left in the first half. Tom Brady would work his two-minute offensive magic with a quick drive that ended with a 22-yard touchdown pass to Gronkowski for the 14-7 lead with 31 seconds left in the half. Wilson, on the other hand, led a short 80-yard drive that included a 17-yard run, a 23-yard pass to Ricardo Lockette, and an 11-yard pass to Chris Matthews for a tying touchdown.

The Patriots found themselves trailing 24-14 after a Wilson touchdown pass to Doug Baldwin and a 27-yard field goal from Steven Hauschka entering the fourth quarter. Brady was determined not to let this Super Bowl get away from him and was able to throw two touchdown passes in the final frame with two long offensive drives that ate up the clock, ending with a 4-yard pass to Danny Amendola and a 3-yard pass to Julian Edelman. But there were still two minutes left for the Seahawks to make one final run, something that Wilson had done throughout the first three seasons of his NFL career.

It was starting to look like Brady would watch the Patriots' defense fall apart as Wilson led a drive to New England's one-yard line. The prevailing thought was that there would be a handoff to Lynch, who has made a career of touchdowns in short yardage situations. But instead, the Seahawks called for a quick slant pass from Wilson to Lockette, which ended up in the hands of rookie cornerback Malcolm Butler in a surprising play that led to a New England win.

The Super Bowl MVP award went to Brady, who completed 37-of-50 passes for 328 yards with four touchdowns despite two interceptions.

But the quarterback handed the keys to the brand new pickup truck provided by one of the game's sponsors to Butler, who won the Vince Lombardi for the Patriots in a quick-reaction play.

While there was no controversy regarding who won between Seattle and New England, the Patriots' victory would be short-lived as the questions from the "Deflate-Gate" controversy would continue, and answers would be found a few months later.

Chapter 7: Deflate-Gate Controversy

The results of the Wells' investigation of the deflated footballs during the AFC Championship game four months prior were released, and the Patriots organization was notified of discipline that would be handed out on May 11. There was a one-million dollar fine for the team plus forfeiture of a first-round pick in the 2016 NFL Draft and a fourth round selection in 2017. But the biggest highlight from the league's statement was the suspension of Brady for the first four regular-season games of the 2015 season without any pay, a big blow to an offense that had depended on the four-time champion quarterback.

According to a news report from the Associated Press a few days before the punishment, the 243-page report essentially labeled Brady a cheater without spelling it out. The report stated that his defense against the claims of having any involvement was implausible and that his refusal to cooperate with the investigation led to the belief that he was, at least in some way, aware of what was going on with regards to footballs being deflated before the Patriots played the Colts. It was probably transpiring in other games as well.

The investigation shows that the two main culprits were two Patriots employees who executed the plan, locker room attendant Jim McNally and equipment assistant John Jastremski. In a series of text messages that were retrieved by the investigation team and a series of interviews, it was found that McNally would take the 12 footballs the Patriots used during the game into a bathroom to let out some air before delivering them to the field. The footballs are usually measured by the officials at halftime but somehow the lost pressure occurred between the official's inspection and the break.

The Associated Press report also mentioned that additional evidence to support the claim includes text messages between McNally and Jastremski in January that implied Brady's request to deflate the footballs and that he had been upset by the past quality of game balls. The text messages also revealed that Brady would throw in some items for the good work, including autographed footballs, jerseys, and other memorabilia.

Brady's numbers seemed to have improved significantly in the second half of the AFC Championship in the Patriots' 45-7 win over Indianapolis. Brady had one touchdown pass in the first quarter while New England led 17-7 at halftime. Brady threw two more touchdown passes, one to Nate Solder for 16 yards and another to Rob Gronkowski for five yards, to extend the lead to 31-7 – two touchdowns from running back LeGarrette Blount for a total of three helped cap off the final score.

After a near interception late in the game, Colts defenders began to notice something was suspicious and talked with officials after the game. Footballs with less air pressure have been known to be easier to catch and grip – conditions that some quarterbacks prefer for better throwing. During a game, each team supplies regulation footballs, and the Associated Press noted that Brady had a significant role in the updated rules that allowed visiting teams to provide the footballs used on offense in 2006.

During the investigation, Brady would not provide access to his emails, text messages, or phone records. But through Jastremski's records, the investigation team found a considerable number of phone calls and text messages between him and the Patriots' quarterback shortly after the people began to talk about the possibility of tampering during the AFC Championship game.

In a letter from NFL Executive President Troy Vincent to Brady, the investigation's report shows that there is enough evidence to conclude that Brady was "at least generally aware of the actions of the Patriots' employees involved … and that it was unlikely that their actions were done without your knowledge." Vincent also points out that Brady's failure to comply with the investigation team's requests for any relevant electronic evidence also played a factor in the decision, all leading to conduct that was considered detrimental to the integrity of the NFL and the sport of football.

"Each player, no matter how accomplished and otherwise respected, has an obligation to comply with the rules and must be held accountable for his actions when those rules are violated, and the public's confidence in the game is called into question," Vincent wrote in his letter that was later released to the public through the NFL's website.

In the following days through NFL Insider reporter Ian Rapoport on Twitter (@RapSheet), Wells had even stated that he told Brady he would not even hold Brady's cell phone. He would just take printouts and that everything private would be kept that way, but Brady still refused to cooperate and led to the speculation that doomed him.

This was not the first time the Patriots were accused of not playing fair. Spygate was the first controversy that revolved around the Patriots being found videotaping defensive signals of the New York Jets during the first game of the 2007 season, but that was more of a violation specifically by head coach Bill Belichick. It was not the only game, however, since it was revealed by the NFL that the Patriots started the practice since Belichick took over in 2000, which included a 35-0 win over the Green Bay Packers.

Multiple reports from various news organizations later found that the information was then transferred to Brady to know what the defense was setting up based on their hand signals, giving Brady a chance to audible into a play that would exploit the defense's weaknesses. Since then, the Patriots had always had a bad reputation surrounded by negative speculations of whether they could win without an unfair advantage.

The NFL officials found that there was no proof that the videotaping had any effect in the four Super Bowls which the Patriots had won since 2000, but there have been doubts among fans, players, and personnel from among the other 31 teams in the league. Former Carolina Panthers general manager Marty Hurney spoke out during an interview with the ESPN 730 AM radio station in Charlotte, North Carolina before Super Bowl XLIX to get his reaction to the recent news, considering that his Panthers lost to the Patriots in 2004 during Super Bowl XXXVIII. To say the least, he questioned whether or not the Patriots had done something that gave them the three-point advantage which led to Carolina's 32-29 loss.

"This is about a culture," he said during the radio broadcast on January 26, 2015. "Is there a culture of cheating at probably what most people look at as the best franchise in the National Football League?"

When the news came out of Brady's suspension, there was a mixed reaction among players in the NFL. Obviously, many of the Patriots were not pleased with the news, with LeGarrette Blount taking to Twitter:

"THIS IS ABSOLUTELY RIDICULOUS!!! SMH. #PATSNATION STAND UP!!!!!" – posted @LG_Blount on May 11, 2015.

Other players outside of the Patriots organization seemed to be sympathetic for Brady as well, including Hall of Fame wide receiver Jerry Rice through his Twitter account @JerryRice: "To win four Super Bowl is outstanding. I know Tom Brady is a great competitor and leader. I feel sorry for him and Patriots nation!"

Maybe that is a big thing to keep in mind about Brady's future legacy. He has still put up numbers that only a few quarterbacks have been able to accomplish. The rules have evolved from the days where there were strict regulations regarding the air pressure in football in the earlier days of the sport. There is also the notion that the filming of teams is usually done through game films that are commonly exchanged between teams to prepare for upcoming opponents. There is always the chance to study defensive setups and hand signals based on past game films from earlier in the season, or at least the most recent film available, considering things like coaching and personnel changes.

Some NFL experts also feel the football's air pressure is not that much of an advantage because the defenders should have just as easy of a time intercepting a pass from Brady as the Patriots' receivers compared to a pass with a football at the league-mandated psi level. It is hard to tell if this will affect Brady's overall standing when he retires and his bid to be selected into the Pro Football Hall of Fame in

Canton, Ohio. There was not anything concerning punishment announced in the first few weeks after the 2014-15 season ended. The tenure of the Belichick-Brady coach-quarterback duo was still expected be able to play the final 12 regular season games of the 2015 season. If they qualified, they would play at the playoffs that help set up Super Bowl 50 to be played February 7, 2016, at Levi's Stadium in Santa Clara, California. It was the home of the San Francisco 49ers, the team Brady grew up watching as a child with top quarterbacks Joe Montana and Steve Young.

Chapter 8: Offseason Legal Battle with NFL

About three months after the Patriots win over the Seattle Seahawks in Super Bowl XLIX, the NFL released an extensive 243-page report about the investigative work done regarding what was being called by many as "Deflate-Gate." Inside the document, the investigative team made the statement that there was at least some awareness of the intentional deflating of footballs during the AFC Championship game.[xxviii] With the findings of the private investigation, the league made the announcement that Brady would be suspended the first four games of the 2015 season because of the evidence, which they considered substantial enough to prove that the quarterback was aware of the team employees changing the air pressure. It also did not help that Brady was not cooperating with the investigation and did not help with answering questions at all.[xxix]

A letter sent to Brady was also published that said the quarterback's actions were considered harmful to the game of football and the league overall.[xxx] It also talked about Brady's unwillingness to cooperate by providing emails, text messages, and other conversations during the day of the 2015 AFC Championship and giving testimony that was not acceptable by the league. It only took about three days before Brady would appeal the suspension through the league's players association – although the commissioner of the NFL Roger Goodell would hear the appeal, despite the NFLPA pushing for a neutral party to oversee it.[xxxi] While it seemed like a conflict of interests, it was part of the collective bargaining agreement made in 2011 to prevent a season being lost to a lockout between the league and the NFLPA.

Two months later, Goodell announced that he would keep Brady's four-game suspension intact, which made several fans worry that the Patriots were going to be without their veteran quarterback for the first four games of the season.[xxxii] In fact, the online searches of New England's backup option, Jimmy Garoppolo, had increased significantly. However, the dispute between Brady and the NFL would have a day in court where Brady gave the NFLPA the green light to have the suspension appealed in a federal courtroom.[xxxiii] Brady made a public statement on his social media accounts where he claimed innocence and that no one within the Patriots' organization was guilty.[xxxiv] He also stated that he was going to dispute what he considered "unfair discipline" so that it would not become a precedent for other players in the league, or at least he would not allow it without a legal fight in a federal courtroom. The opinions were mixed between NFL writers, analysts, and legal experts.

On the one hand, many felt that the punishment was extremely harsh but fair. Others also felt that the league finally caught the Patriots shady play after several years of controversy involving the "Spy-gate" during the Super Bowl matchup with the St. Louis Rams back in 2002 and other instances where the Patriots were accused of bending the rules. At the same time, considering Brady guilty was more based on how he did not cooperate with the investigation and less with hard evidence at the time. There were text messages from other sources, but nothing that ultimately linked the New England quarterback.

In the meantime, Garoppolo was getting a lot of the snaps during the preseason in the event that Brady's suspension would still be kept. While the appeal was going to the federal court, Brady was still practicing with the team and keeping himself ready for the 2015 NFL season. But the Patriots wanted to evaluate what they had with their backup who was drafted from Eastern Illinois University in 2014. He struggled a little in a 22-11 preseason loss to the Green Bay Packers where he completed 20 of 30 for 159 yards and one interception. He improved in the second game in New Orleans with 28 of 33 for 269 yards and a touchdown during a 26-24 win, followed by completing 13 out of 17 for 126 yards and another touchdown for a 17-16 win over Carolina.

One week before the start of the regular season, the appeal was heard in federal court, and the man who oversaw the case was Judge Richard M. Berman, an established judge of the Federal District Court in Manhattan, New York. While the suspension was for the deflation of footballs in the AFC Championship, the judge was more focused on the fact that Goodell was given the authority to both hand out the suspension and then oversee the appeal hearing months later. This brought into question the fairness and objectiveness of the matter.[xxxv] Berman made the decision that the suspension would be lifted because of several "legal deficiencies" in the case and that Brady was not given a fair appeals case back in July 2015. In addition to that, the court found that Brady had no awareness he could be suspended for the matter because "general awareness" is not within the NFL policies, nor was there a precedent set from previous suspensions. The league never had a situation where a player was obstructing an investigation. All of this allowed Brady to be eligible to play in the season-opening game on September 10, 2015, against the Pittsburgh Steelers to kick off the NFL season.

The league was not happy and announced that they were going to appeal Berman's decision through their legal action. It has not helped Goodell's credibility in the league with many people believing that he should no longer have the power to oversee appeals, which was recently a discussion during NFLPA meetings with the league officials. But it was going to be a while before there would be any action taken in court since the league was probably going to take their time to prepare their appeal that would be held after the 2015-16 NFL season. It was going to feature the 50th anniversary of the Super Bowl, and the league needed to focus on promoting the golden anniversary of their championship game, one that Brady was hoping he would participate in for his fifth championship.

Chapter 9: 2015-16 Season, Climbing Numbers[xxxvi]

When quarterbacks start getting closer to age 40, production usually starts to fall a little bit. But Brady did not have much of a decrease in his skills. There also might have been a chance that Brady had some frustration built up from the legal battle with the NFL. The unfortunate recipients of that released frustration were the Pittsburgh Steelers during the season opener on September 10, 2015. Brady completed a 16-yard pass to tight end Rob Gronkowski early in the second quarter and then led another touchdown drive with a six-yard pass to Gronkowski before halftime. Brady would have two more touchdowns in a game where they were able to outlast the Pittsburgh offense for a 28-21 win. Brady completed 25 out of 32 passes for 288 yards. The win over Pittsburgh also gave Brady the league record for the most wins with one team as it was Brady's 161st win during his time with the New England Patriots.[xxxvii]

The momentum continued on September 20, 2015. Brady would once again put up monster numbers with 38 completions out of 59 attempts to finish with 466 yards and three touchdowns – two of which went to wide receiver Julian Edelman for eight yards in the first quarter and another for 22 yards in the late third quarter. While the Bills had a small comeback in the fourth quarter, kicker Stephen Gostkowski helped secure the 40-32 win late in the game. Brady then followed those first two dominating performance with another over the

Jacksonville Jaguars during a 51-17 win on September 27, 2015. He had 33 completions for 358 yards for two touchdowns to Danny Amendola for one yard before the end of the first half and then a 13-yard pass to Keshawn Martin near the end of the third quarter. Most of the Patriots' 51 points came from LeGarrette Blount having three touchdowns with 78 yards.

On October 11, 2015, Brady would have another impressive game, making 20 completions out of 27 (74.1 completion percentage) for 275 yards and two touchdowns during a 30-6 win at Dallas. Brady's top play came on a 59-yard pass to Edelman for a score to start the fourth quarter. It is hard to imagine how the Patriots would have played in these four games if Brady was forced to serve that suspension that a federal court dismissed, but the folks in Pittsburgh, Buffalo, Jacksonville, and Dallas would have wished for a chance to play the backup Jimmy Garoppolo. During New England's first four games, Brady had nearly 1,400 passing yards with 11 touchdowns, no interceptions, and a completion rate of about 72.5 percent – all adding up to a quarterback rating of about 121.5.

The winning streak continued with a 34-27 win on October 18, 2015, in a road win over Indianapolis where Brady completed 23 of 37 for 312 yards and three touchdowns in a shootout with Andrew Luck, who had 312 yards and three touchdowns of his own. Brady's perfect touchdown to interception ratio was ended as he threw an interception to Colts' defensive back Mike Adams and it was returned for a touchdown. Brady would go back to his dominant nature with 355 yards and two touchdowns during a 30-23 win at home against the New York Jets on October 25, 2015. This was followed by having 356 yards and four touchdowns in a 36-7 win over the Miami Dolphins on October 29, 2015, giving him more than 700 yards and six touchdowns in a four-day gap.

The Patriots started the season with ten straight wins. But throughout the streak, many injuries impacted the New England office, including Edelman, Amendola, Aaron Dobson, and running back Dion Lewis. The streak ended November 29, 2015, during a 30-24 loss. Brady played well for most of the game when he had 280 yards and three touchdown passes on just 23 completions. One of those touchdowns was to Gronkowski for 23 yards and the other on a deep 63-yard pass to Brandon Bolden. However, Brady lost another target late in the fourth quarter when suffered an injury to his right knee after a legal hit by Denver safety Darian Stewart knocked the Patriots' tight end out of the game.[xxxviii] The Broncos would complete the fourth quarter comeback with 17 unanswered points that forced the Patriots to tie the game on a 47-yard field goal as the time expired in overtime. Denver's C.J. Anderson had a 48-yard touchdown run to help the Broncos hand New England their first loss of the season by a score of 30-24.

New England struggled in the final five games of the regular season as they would lose three of those games to finish the season with a record of 12-4. Brady was still putting up some big numbers for the season with a 64.4 completion percent to have 4,770 yards with 36 touchdowns, and he had only seven interceptions in the 2015-16 season. The worst game he had was on December 6, 2015, during a 35-28 loss where he completed just 29 out of 56 throws for 312 yards with three touchdowns, but two interceptions. So despite the injury problems, the Patriots were still able to finish well enough to win the AFC East Division crown while earning the second seed in the AFC playoff standings. They lost the head-to-head tiebreaker over the 12-4 Broncos and had the tiebreaker over the 12-4 Cincinnati Bengals due to having a higher winning percentage against common opponents.

The Patriots would face the Kansas City Chiefs, who were on a roll after winning ten games to end the regular season and had defeated the Houston Texans on the road, 30-0, during the AFC Wild Card Playoffs. The Chiefs gave New England a tough game, but the Patriots had some key players return to the lineup from injury just in time for the playoffs. Brady was glad to have Gronkowski back as they connected on an eight-yard touchdown early in the first quarter. Brady also had a goal-line touchdown in the second quarter to mount a 14-6 lead at halftime. Brady would complete another touchdown for 16 yards to Gronkowski, while the Chiefs would get a couple of goals, but were not able to finalize the comeback with a 27-20 win to set up another matchup between Brady and his rival Peyton Manning in the AFC Championship and a sense of déjà vu for the NFL fans.

On January 24, 2016, Manning looked okay in the game, but he was not at his best due to injuries suffered earlier in the regular season. He completed 17 of 32 for 176 yards and two touchdowns from the first half of the game. Brady struggled as he threw two interceptions in the game while completing just 27 out of 56 total passes for 310 yards. Brady and the New England offense would get a chance to tie the game as Brady led a two-minute offense where he had a deep 40-yard pass to Gronkowski on fourth down, which would help set up a four-yard touchdown pass to Gronkowski to make the score 20-18. Brady would try to complete a pass to Edelman on a two-point conversion attempt, but could not connect, and the Broncos were able to survive as they advanced to Super Bowl 50 where the defense was able to handle the Carolina Panthers for the 24-10 win.

It was a tough ending for the season for Brady and the Patriots, a team that had a hot start in the regular season before injuries began to impact Brady's number of targets in the second half of the season. Nonetheless, the team felt that they could improve for the next year and try to help Brady get that fifth Super Bowl championship.

Chapter 10: Deflate-Gate Part II, Contract Extension

A few weeks after Super Bowl 50 concluded, the Patriots decided to give Brady a contract extension that would last through the 2019 NFL season, according to ESPN NFL insiders Adam Schefter and Dianna Russini[xxxix]. This meant that Brady would be playing in the NFL until he was 42 and he would be the third player in league history to spend at least 20 seasons with the same team. The first was offensive lineman Jackie Slater, who spent 20 seasons with the Los Angeles Rams organization and his final year when the team moved to St. Louis, Missouri, and the second was Darrel Green, who played 20 seasons as a defensive back with the Washington Redskins. It was exciting news as people were speculating at the time whether his long-time rival Peyton Manning was going to retire after he had played his 18th season in the NFL and won his second NFL Championship at Super Bowl 50.

But Brady probably helped the Patriots as well since he was expected to make about $15 million in 2016 in the previous contract that was for only two more seasons through the 2016 and 2017 seasons. But the Patriots were also hoping to use some of the space they would have in the salary cap to make sure they signed key defensive starters to long-term contracts – i.e. Dont'a Hightower and Malcolm Butler. Brady turned 39 years old before the start of the 2016 NFL season, but his numbers in 2015 indicate that he is not about to slow down right away. In fact, he set the league record for touchdown to interception ratio for a quarterback age 38 or older with 5.1 touchdowns for every interception; beating out Brett Favre's 4.7 touchdowns to one interception in the 2009 season with the Minnesota Vikings.

But there are rumors that the contract extension will likely help reduce the amount of money Brady might lose if he does suffer a suspension at the beginning of the 2016 season. It was only a matter of days after the contract extension announcement that the league announced they were officially filing an appeal of Judge Richard M. Berman's decision to dismiss the four-game suspension that Brady was initially meant to serve. He was supposed to serve his suspension at the beginning of the 2015 season due to the role he played in the Deflate-Gate controversy from the 2015 AFC Championship against the Indianapolis Colts, which sent Brady to Super Bowl XLIX to defeat the Seattle Seahawks for his fourth championship.[xl]

Because of the victory of the appealed suspension back in September 2015, several legal experts felt that Brady and the NFL Players Association held the advantage in the upcoming hearing for the NFL's appeal of Berman's decision. Michael McCann of Sports Illustrated said the potential outcome is based on the track records of the three judges that are selected by the U.S Court of Appeals' Second Circuit for a panel that will host the hearing – Robert Katzmann, Barrington Parker, Jr., and Danny Chin.[xli]

However, that advantage never came to fruition. The April ruling against Brady was more of the affirmation of Goodell's powers as NFL commissioner granted through the collective bargaining agreement than it was conclusive proof Brady did any wrongdoing. The saga had finally come to an end: Tom Brady was going to serve a four-game suspension to start the 2016 season.

Brady made that official in mid-July when he announced that he would not appeal the ruling, which would have made it a potential case for the United States Supreme Court to hear.

His decision brought to an end a saga that was one of the most unique situations in the history of the NFL and professional sports overall. It was unprecedented for a football player who has had a disputed suspension garner this much attention from the legal community.

The 2016 Season

With the ruling being given in April and Brady's decision not to appeal the suspension during training camp, the Patriots had the entire training camp and preseason to prepare Garoppolo for the first part of the season. Brady was allowed to practice with the team throughout the preseason and play in preseason games, but once the calendar moved to the regular season, the future Hall of Famer would not be around the Patriots complex.

Not that they missed him all that much in the first four weeks of the season. New England went 3-1 in Brady's absence, even after needing to turn to third-string quarterback and rookie Jacoby Brissett after Garoppolo went down with a shoulder injury in the Patriots' Week 2 victory over Miami. The defense made things life easy for Brissett on a short turnaround as New England waxed Houston 27-0 in a Thursday night game, but the rookie signal-caller was out of his depth against Rex Ryan and the Buffalo Bills, going just 1 for 12 on third down in a 16-0 defeat to their AFC East rivals.

But all things considered, the Patriots were in great shape for Brady's return. They already held their customary spot atop the division and trailed only the Denver Broncos for the best record in the conference. On Monday, October 4, Brady's suspension officially ended and it was time to get back to business.

"I'm going to take it day to day," Brady told Jim Gray in an interview with Westwood One Radio on his first day back. "My teammates have been working their butts off, and that's what they expect of me. I'll take the days as they come. I'll certainly need the practices to try and get on the (same) page as all the guys who have been practicing the last four weeks. But I'm really looking forward to it."

While stepping into the starting quarterback's job is never easy, whether returning from injury or suspension, Brady could not have asked for a better first opponent than the Cleveland Browns. They had given up at least 25 points in every game during their 0-4 start, and a porous defense had yielded ten touchdown passes in those games.

After the defense had forced a three-and-out on the game's first possession, it was time for Brady to take the field for the first time in 2016. Any thoughts he would need to scrape off the rust were quickly erased when he completed a 10-yard pass to Edelman and a 19-yarder to Gronkowski on his first two plays from scrimmage. Brady and Gronkowski hooked up again later in the drive on a 34-yard pass play that set up Blount's 1-yard touchdown run that opened the scoring.

The Browns promptly tied the game on their next possession, and Brady answered again as he directed the Patriots 75 yards. This time he capped the drive with his first touchdown pass of the season, a seven-yarder to Martellus Bennett that gave New England a 14-7 advantage with 2:12 left in the first quarter.

The third possession was more of the same. Brady directed the offense like he never missed a snap. A 43-yard pass to Chris Hogan keyed another touchdown drive capped by a second TD toss to Bennett. By this point, Brady was 13 for 15 for 185 yards, and the two incompletions were the result of drops by his receivers. It was now 23-7 early in the second quarter, and the only blemish in the first half was the Browns making a goal-line stand as Blount was stuffed twice from the 1-yard line on consecutive plays.

Brady threw his third and final touchdown pass of the game to finish off New England's first possession of the second half. Again it was Bennett, as the tight end hauled in a 37-yard scoring pass. New England would eventually win the game 33-13, and for a guy who had not practiced for a month before his suspension, Brady looked awfully good. He completed 28 of 40 passes for 406 yards, did not throw an interception, and took only one sack that resulted in a three-yard loss. He spread the wealth as seven different receivers caught at least two passes, and the Patriots served notice that they were most certainly Super Bowl contenders once more. But after the game, Brady was all business, just like his coach and the Patriots always were under Belichick.

"This isn't the time for me to reflect," he told The New York Times. "I've just moved on, man."

Next up for Brady would be his highly anticipated home season debut against the Cincinnati Bengals. While the Bengals put up more resistance than the Browns, they were having a hard time getting to Brady. The Patriots' defense also helped the cause with a goal-line stand in the second quarter, but the game finally opened up late in the first half when the Bengals took a 7-3 lead on a 2-yard scramble by quarterback Andy Dalton.

Brady shook off a sack and was aided by an illegal contact penalty by the Bengals on a 3rd-and-18 that kept the drive alive. He then masterfully conducted a two-minute offense, ripping off five straight completions and capping the drive with a 15-yard TD toss to James White to put New England back on top.

Cincinnati would score on the first possession of the second half, but the defense again answered the challenge, this time recording a safety to cut the deficit to 14-12. On the ensuing possession, Brady directed a five-play, 68-yard drive that ended with a four-yard flip to Gronkowski. The Patriots forced a three-and-out, and it took Brady only four plays to go 53 yards, and his four-yard TD toss to White provided a 25-14 lead as they coasted to a 35-17 win.

It was two games and two wins for Brady, who had completed 57 of 75 passes for 782 yards and six touchdowns without an interception. His masterful use of Gronkowski and Bennett in New England's two tight-end formations in the middle of the field had opened up seams for Edelman and Hogan to do damage on the perimeter. But Brady and the Patriots were taking a step up in weight class for Week 7 as they traveled to Pittsburgh for a contest against the Steelers. But Steelers coach Mike Tomlin would be without his starting quarterback as Ben Roethlisberger was sidelined with a knee injury, leaving Landry Jones as Brady's counterpart for this game.

With Jones, the Steelers hung tough. Brady and Jones traded first-half touchdown passes, and the Steelers had closed within 14-13 at 8:44 of the third quarter after a 46-yard field goal by Chris Boswell. Here, though, was where Blount and Brady shined. Blount bulled his way for 36 yards on the first two plays of the drive, and Brady delivered a 36-yard strike over the middle to Gronkowski that restored New England's lead to 20-13. Pittsburgh countered with a field goal, but now it was Brady making the big plays like his 37-yard toss to Gronkowski set up a five-yard scamper by Blount to give the Patriots a 27-16 win.

"It was good to score like that and good to make plays in the second half we needed to," Brady said after his team improved to 6-1. "They certainly made it tough on us."

The midpoint of New England's season brought a trip to Buffalo to face the Bills and a chance to avenge their 16-0 loss at home in Week 4. Rex Ryan has never hidden how much he enjoys trying to match wits with Belichick and Brady, but this was also the last real challenge the Patriots had in the division. Win this game, and New England would enjoy a three-game lead atop the AFC East and have the inside track to the top seed in the conference.

For his part, Brady has used the Bills as a personal whipping post and carried a 25-3 career record against them into the game. It would be quickly apparent that win number 26 would take place in upstate New York. Brady had a pair of first-quarter touchdown passes, including a 53-yarder to Hogan, as the Pats raced to a 14-3 lead. Following a Bills touchdown, New England scored 24 points in a 16:13 span bridging halftime to blow out Buffalo. Brady had a pair of touchdown passes, including one to Gronkowski that made him the Patriots all-time leader in receiving touchdowns, and Blount finished the surge with a 1-yard plunge as New England cruised to a 41-25 win.

Brady's numbers continued to be mind-boggling. He was 22 of 33 for 315 yards and four touchdowns without an interception versus Buffalo and had thrown for 1,319 yards and 12 touchdowns without being picked off since his return. His passer rating was a gaudy 133.9

– a perfect rating is 158.3 – and his completion percentage was a robust 73.1 percent.

About the only thing that could slow Brady down was the bye, which came in Week 9. But it also gave him and the Patriots a week to prepare for a nationally-televised Sunday Night Football home game against the Seattle Seahawks. It was the first time the teams had played since the Patriots' late interception sealed Brady's fourth title in Super Bowl XLIX.

The game more than lived up to the hype in a bruising, physical contest. At one point, Seahawks safety Earl Thomas crushed Gronkowski with a legal hit as the tight end tried to catch a pass over the middle. While Gronkowski would return to the game after getting the wind knocked out of him, it would start the process of a recurring back injury that would eventually end the tight end's season early.

The game went back and forth and featured five lead changes in the first three quarters. While Brady did not have a touchdown pass, he was effectively moving the Patriots, and Blount was finishing off drives by getting into the end zone on three occasions.

Seattle, though, was also a championship-caliber team and refused to yield. The teams traded field goals before Wilson and Doug Baldwin combined on a 15-yard touchdown pass to make it 31-24 with 4:24 to play. Seahawks coach Pete Carroll aggressively went for a two-point conversion to make it a two-possession game, but Wilson's pass fell incomplete and gave Brady a chance to at least force overtime with a touchdown.

Three completions moved the ball to midfield, and a 30-yard pass to Edelman on 3rd-and-8 put the Patriots at the Seahawks 24 by the two-minute warning. After Blount had been tripped up for a four-yard loss, Brady found Gronkowski for a 26-yard gain to the Seattle 2 with 89 seconds left. Brady tried a sneak up the middle but gained only one yard.

Blount was then denied on second down, and the clock was down to 19 seconds before the Pats called timeout. Brady again called his number but never had full control of the ball before falling on his fumble at the 2. The Seahawks were whistled for having too many men on the field, setting up a 4th-and-goal from the 1 with 14 seconds left. And in a reversal of fortune from Super Bowl XLIX, it was the Seahawks who made a successful goal-line stand as Brady's fourth-down pass for Gronkowski was well-defended by Kam Chancellor and left the Patriots on the short end of a 31-24 scoreline.

Brady and the Pats would try to bounce back in San Francisco, marking the first time in his career he would play in the Bay Area, where as a child he rooted for the 49ers. Looking every bit the part of Joe Montana, his boyhood idol, Brady came out hot by completing his first eight passes. San Francisco hung around and trailed 13-10 after three quarters, but TD passes to Amendola and Malcolm Mitchell in a

4:49 span early in the fourth quarter powered the Patriots to a 30-17 victory.

Brady finished with 280 yards and four touchdown passes, his day capped by a rainbow that appeared over Levis Stadium.

"It was very cool," said Brady in one of the few times he let his guard down all season. "It doesn't get any better than that. To have the first chance ever to do that was very special. I felt it in pregame warmup, and it carried right to the last play of the game. It was pretty great.

"They (the 49ers) have a great organization, they always have. They inspired a lot of kids here in the Bay Area in my time growing up, and I was one of them."

After a pleasant cross-country flight back east, the Patriots would play their division rivals, the New York Jets, on the road. The Jets always seem to provide scrappy resistance at home against Brady, and this game was no different. New York grabbed a 17-13 lead in the fourth quarter with 10:17 to play on a 22-yard TD pass by Ryan Fitzpatrick.

Brady directed a drive that cut the deficit to one with a field goal, and after the Pats had made a defensive stand, he had the ball at his own 17 with 5:04 to play. Passes to Edelman and Dion Lewis gained 40 yards, but the Patriots faced a 4th-and-4 at the Jets' 37 with 3:30 to play. Brady calmly found White for a four-yard gain that moved the chains and then hooked up with Hogan for 25 yards. On the first play after the two-minute warning, Brady found Mitchell from eight yards out, and New England escaped with a 22-17 win. The victory, though, came at a cost as it was revealed that Gronkowski would miss the rest of the season due to a back injury.

The Patriots made quick work of the Los Angeles Rams, improving to 10-2 with a 26-10 victory as Brady threw for 269 yards and a touchdown. He shredded Baltimore for 406 yards and three touchdowns the following week, helping New England build a 23-3 lead as they hung on for a 30-23 victory. Brady also threw his 450th touchdown pass in the win, making him just the fourth quarterback to reach that milestone.

Week 15 had the Patriots traveling to Denver to face the Broncos. While they were a different team following the retirement of quarterback Peyton Manning, the Broncos still boasted a standout defensive unit and were contending for the AFC West title. It was also a chance for the Patriots to avenge their conference title game loss to the Broncos from January.

In that game, the Broncos had their way with the Patriots offensive line and battered Brady to the tune of 23 hits. This time around, a stronger offensive line and the consistent running game Lewis and Blount provided gave the Patriots a better balance.

Brady had a rare slow start, misfiring on his first six passes as the defenses had the upper hand early. The teams traded first-quarter field goals before an interception in the red zone by Ryan Logan blunted a Broncos drive, and his 46-yard return gave Brady excellent field position. New England capitalized with Brady and Edelman hooking up three times for 45 yards before Blount bulled his way over from the 1 for a 10-3 Patriots lead.

It would turn out to be the only touchdown of the game as the Patriots stifled the Broncos. Gostkowski added a pair of second-half field goals, and the result was a 16-3 victory that not only gave New England their eighth consecutive AFC East title, but also a first-round bye into the divisional round.

Brady and the Patriots had an early Christmas present as they played a Jets team that was playing out the string of a miserable season. Brady had thrown three first-half touchdown passes before Blount had a pair of short scoring runs as New England pasted New York 41-3 and held the Jets to 239 total yards.

But home-field advantage throughout the playoffs still had not been secured. New England still needed a victory at Miami to make sure the road in the AFC playoffs traveled through Foxborough. And once more, Brady and the Patriots left no doubt about the outcome. He threw TD passes to Bennett and Michael Floyd 3:44 apart in the first quarter, and a 77-yard scoring play to Edelman in the third quarter provided more than enough offense for a 35-14 win. New England finished 14-2 and became just the ninth team since 1972 to go undefeated on the road.

Despite missing four games, Brady still had an impressive season statistically. He threw for 3,554 yards and 28 touchdowns with only two interceptions. He completed 67.4 percent of his passes, and his 112.2 passer rating was the second-highest of his career, behind only his 117.2 mark from 2007. Brady was rightfully among those considered for the NFL Most Valuable Player award, but it eventually went to Atlanta Falcons quarterback Matt Ryan in what turned out to be a foreshadowing of things to come.

The Patriots got to watch the wild-card round unfold and learned their divisional round opponent would be the Houston Texans, who beat an Oakland Raiders team that lost starting quarterback Derek Carr to a season-ending leg injury late in the regular season.

The AFC South champions had totaled just 25 touchdowns during the regular season, three less than Brady had in four fewer games. Still, the playoffs are about survival and not turning the ball over to advance. New England had a chance to blow open the game after Lewis' 98-yard kickoff return provided a 14-3 lead late in the first quarter, but turnovers on back-to-back possessions allowed the Texans to score 10 points in a 45-second span and pull within 14-13 on a 10-yard touchdown pass from Brock Osweiler in the second quarter.

Brady was able to lead the Patriots to a late first-half field goal, but the game was still up for grabs. On the second possession of the third quarter, Brady found Edelman on consecutive plays for 40 yards to get to midfield, and the two would hook up again two more times on quick 7-yard passes. The Patriots would extend their lead to 24-13 on

Brady's 19-yard scoring pass to White, but they still could not put away the game as Brady was picked off on the final play of the third quarter.

The Texans, though, could only turn that into three points. Osweiler was then picked off by Ryan, who returned it to the Houston 6. Two plays later, Lewis scored his third touchdown of the game, sealing a 34-16 win and a sixth consecutive trip to the AFC title game. Brady, though, was far from pleased with his performance despite finishing with 287 yards and two TD passes.

"Whoever we play next week is going to be a great football team," he said. "We're going to have to play better than we played tonight on offense."

That whoever would turn out to be the Pittsburgh Steelers, who ground their way past the Kansas City Chiefs with six field goals in an 18-16 road victory. This time, Roethlisberger would be under center for Pittsburgh, but the critical injury came during the game as running back Le'Veon Bell suffered a strained groin in the first quarter.

Bell's injury notwithstanding, Brady was simply not going to be denied. He got the Pats off to a quick 3-0 lead on their opening drive and was finding creases throughout Pittsburgh's defense. That resulted in a 16-yard scoring toss to Hogan as the lead grew to 10-0 late in the first quarter.

Bell's last snap would come two plays later, but backup DeAngelo Williams shouldered the load and pulled the Steelers within 10-6 on a five-yard touchdown run with 11:37 before halftime. It would, however, be as close as Pittsburgh would get on this day. Brady and Hogan hooked up again, this time on a 34-yard flea-flicker to make it 17-6. While the Steelers had the ball for the next six minutes, they could only manage a field goal. New England led 17-9 at halftime and was 30 minutes away from the Super Bowl.

Gostkowski restored the 11-point lead with a 47-yard field goal to cap the Patriots' first possession of the second half, and Brady sapped the life out of the Steelers with an eight-play, 88-yard drive – keyed by a 39-yard pass to Hogan – that Blount finished with a 1-yard TD. The Steelers turned the ball over two plays later, and it took four plays for Brady to find Edelman for a 10-yard TD toss.

It was 33-9 and all but certain: Tom Brady and the Patriots were going to the Super Bowl for the seventh time in his illustrious career. After the 36-17 win, the talk from Brady was not about redemption for "Deflate-Gate" or anything of that nature; it was about being the best teammate he could be – still the core of what has made Brady and the Patriots successful for now almost two decades running.

"This is my motivation right here, all these fellas in front of me, these guys," Brady said, referring to his teammates. "We won a lot of different ways under a lot of different circumstances. Mental toughness is what it is all about, and this team has got it. We'll see if we can write the perfect ending."

Las Vegas oddsmakers made the Patriots a 3-point favorite against the Falcons for Super Bowl 51. The over-under was established at 57.5 points, meaning they expected an offensive shootout. This made sense given both teams' proficient offenses, with the Falcons also impressively advancing to the Super Bowl by drilling the Green Bay Packers 44-21 in the NFC title game.

The talk leading up to the title game in Houston was about Brady cementing his legacy as the greatest quarterback of all-time with a potential fifth Super Bowl ring. While Ryan won the MVP award, more people viewed it as more motivational fuel for Brady's playing rage than rewarding Ryan for a breakout season that pushed the Falcons to their second Super Bowl appearance in franchise history.

But two weeks of being shunted aside for all that Brady talk created an inner rage for the Falcons. Any thoughts about whether the Falcons belonged on football's biggest stage were quickly erased on their first play from scrimmage as Devonta Freeman scampered 37 yards after the Patriots had pinned Atlanta on its 8-yard line. While the drive did not result in any points, it served notice that Ryan and the Falcons had come to play.

Fifteen minutes passed without a point by either team. The Patriots were trying to put a drive together, but Blount finished on a carry up the middle, and the Falcons recovered on their own 29. Ryan pounced, hitting Julio Jones on consecutive plays for 42 yards. Then it was Freeman gashing the Pats defense for 24 yards on two carries. The Patriots called a timeout to settle down, but it did not help as Freeman took a handoff, bounced outside to the left, and went into the end zone untouched.

Brady went three-and-out, burning just 90 seconds off the clock, and the Falcons pressed aggressively. Ryan quickly got the Falcons in the red zone, and three plays later, he found Austin Hooper on a seam route in the end zone, and it was now 14-0 with 8:55 left in the second quarter.

On the ensuing drive, Brady finally found a rhythm and converted three third downs along the way. He got as far as the Atlanta 23, but on a 3rd-and-6, Brady tried to force a pass into a tight space for Amendola. Robert Alford stepped in front of the pass and raced 82 yards in the opposite direction, giving the Falcons a 21-0 lead with 2:21 to play in the first half.

Now it was a desperate situation. The largest deficit overcome in Super Bowl history was 10 points, and now the Patriots were in a hole more than double that. Brady stopped the bleeding with a two-minute drive that resulted in a 41-yard field goal by Gostkowski that made it 21-3 at halftime. The teams traded empty possessions to start the third quarter before Ryan again found holes to exploit in the Pats defense. He completed a pair of passes to Taylor Gabriel for 52 yards, which helped set up a six-yard toss to Tevin Coleman that extended Atlanta's lead to 28-3 with 8:36 left in the third quarter.

There are no game plans to overcome a 25-point deficit, regardless of coach and regardless of team. The game then becomes about pride and willpower, to make one play at a time and try to stack them one on top of the other and build some momentum. And in that area, this is where the Patriots were the most fortunate team to have Tom Brady directing their offense.

Brady was using a hurry-up offense, but the Falcons did a good job keeping them to short gains as they played a zone defense. It took more than six minutes, but Brady, who kept the drive alive with a 15-yard scramble on 3rd-and-8, found White in the left flat. He turned inside and dove into the end zone to complete a five-yard scoring play. But Gostkowski bounced the extra point off the right upright, leaving the Patriots down 28-9 with 2:06 left in the third quarter.

The Falcons went three-and-out, and Brady went back to work. A bevy of short passes got the Patriots to the Falcons 7, but Atlanta's defense recorded two sacks in three plays, forcing New England to settle for a 33-yard field goal to make it 28-12 with 9:44 to go.

Every comeback needs one key defensive play that bolsters hopes, and the Patriots got it on the next possession. Dont'a Hightower sacked Ryan, forcing a fumble that was recovered by Alan Branch at the Falcons 25. Brady absorbed a sack on the first play but responded with four straight completions, the last a six-yard square-out to

Amendola for a touchdown. White bulled his way in for the two-point conversion, and all of a sudden, it was 28-20 Falcons with 5:56 to play.

Now England opted against an onside kick and pinned Atlanta at its own 10. But Ryan and Freeman hooked up on a 39-yard completion to move the ball to midfield. Two plays later, Ryan and Jones hooked up on a 22-yard completion that would have flattened most opponents. Ryan stepped through pressure in the pocket and fired a pass to the right sideline where Jones made a leaping catch while having the presence of mind to tap both his feet down inbounds before falling out.

The play moved the Falcons into field goal range at the Patriots 22 with 4:40 to go. Freeman lost a yard on first down, but the bigger play was Ryan absorbing a 12-yard sack that moved them back to the 35. A holding penalty scuttled any chance of a field goal, forcing Atlanta to punt. Matt Bosher, though, did his job and pinned New England at its own 9 with 3:30 to play.

Ninety-one yards and a two-point conversion were needed by the Patriots to keep this game alive. It started ominously with a pair of incompletions, but Brady kept the drive going with a 16-yard completion to Hogan. After another incompletion, Brady picked up 11 yards on a pass to Mitchell and another 23 on a completion to Edelman.

Edelman's catch saved the day as the ball was initially tipped by Alford, but it hit his shin as he was falling and Edelman somehow had the presence of mind to grab the ball before it hit the ground. The Falcons challenged the completion, partly to rest a now-exhausted defense, but the call stood and put the ball at the Atlanta 41.

Brady continued his relentless march, hooking up with Amendola on a 20-yard pass. The two-minute warning came three seconds late but with the Patriots in prime position at the Falcons 21. Two plays led to two completions to White and 20 yards down to the 1-yard line. It made sense to reward the running back, and White slipped through a hole into the end zone to make it 28-26 with 57 seconds to go. Using an empty backfield and a five-wide set, Brady called for an inside screen and fired a quick pass to Amendola, who got into the end zone for the tying points.

A 25-point deficit had been overcome. The Patriots now had to hold out one last time to take their chances in overtime. They pinned the Falcons at their own 11, and after four plays, the Patriots forced a punt. One play later, the Super Bowl was heading into unchartered territory for the first time since its inception.

Overtime.

New England had all the momentum on its side as running the hurry-up offense left Atlanta's defense dragging. There is admittedly some humor from the outside that an overtime coin toss is one Belichick wants to win so he can make a choice to receive the kickoff as opposed to deferring the opening toss to receive to start the second half.

The Patriots won the toss and started at their own 25 after a touchback. Once more, it was Brady at the forefront. He completed five straight passes – first to White for six yards, then Amendola for 14. Next was Hogan for 18 and a swing pass to White that resulted in a loss of three yards. He quickly regrouped and found Edelman for a 15-yard gain to the Falcons 25.

White bounced off for a 10-yard run, and then De'Vondre Campbell was called for defensive pass interference, moving the ball to the Falcons 2. After failing to hook up with Bennett on 1st-and goal, Brady called for a running play. He pitched right to White, The running back angled for the sidelines before cutting back inside, and was able to cross the plane of the goal line as he was being tackled.

Less than four minutes after the first overtime in Super Bowl history kicked off, it was over. New England emerged with a 34-28 victory that resulted in a series of rewrites to the Super Bowl record book. The first among them was Brady becoming the first quarterback to win five titles and becoming the second player to win five Super Bowls along with defensive lineman Charles Haley.

He also became the first player to win four Super Bowl MVP honors and set single-game records with 466 passing yards, 43 completions, and 62 attempts. He also set career Super Bowl marks in completions

(207), passing yards (2,071), passing touchdowns (15), and games played (7).

From when the Patriots trailed 28-3, Brady went 26 of 33 for 283 yards as he led them on five scoring drives around a one-play possession that ended regulation.

"We played our tails off to get to this point in the season," Brady said. "To get down 28-3, it was just a lot of mental toughness by our team, and we're all going to remember this for the rest of our lives."

"He was laser-focused, and the entire time, there wasn't a time where we looked at Tom like he knew this thing was over," Hogan said. "There wasn't a doubt in my mind. We have one of the best quarterbacks that ever played the game."

Chapter 11: How Does Brady Rank in NFL History?

Brady and his rival Peyton Manning have both held some high numbers during their time in the league. Both are the only quarterbacks in NFL history to have 50 passing touchdowns in a regular season. For Brady, it was part of the 2007 season where he looked almost unstoppable with 4,806 yards and only eight interceptions as part of a 16-0 regular season. The only blemish that season was the Super Bowl loss to the New York Giants. It is just one of more than 30 individual career records that Brady either owns outright or has a share of in a tie. That 2007 season where the Patriots almost completed a perfect season gave Brady the most regular-season and postseason wins in a single season by any NFL quarterback.

Overall, Brady has been one of the winningest quarterbacks who has stayed with one franchise. While he surpassed Brett Favre's record for most wins with one team at the beginning of the 2015 season, the numbers that currently sit at 183 in the regular season and 208 overall will climb higher considering Brady's most recent contract extension takes him into playing through the 2019 NFL season. He will also likely build onto the all-time passing records as well.

Brady currently sits fourth all-time in passing yards with 61,582 yards. First place is the recently retired Peyton Manning with 71,940, followed by Favre's 71,838 and Drew Brees' 66,111 through the 2016 season.[xlii] Brees could very well end up as the game's all-time leader in passing yards when he decides to retire, and Brady could have an excellent chance of quickly supplanting him when that happens.

The next few seasons should be interesting between Brady and Brees, whose 465 TD passes are good for third place and nine better than Brady heading into the 2017 season. First place is also held by Manning's 539, followed by Favre's 508.

Unlike Manning, Favre, and Marino, Brady has more success in the playoffs. On a side note, Brady has more Super Bowl rings (five) than the three quarterbacks combined – Manning has two, Favre has one, and Marino has never won a Super Bowl. Brady has the most playoff starts, 34, than any other quarterback in the league and has won 25 of those games. During those 34 games, he leads the league in the most touchdown passes (63), passing yards (9,094), completions (831), attempts (1,325) and has made more conference championship starts than anyone else in the league with 11 – he has won the most with seven. Brady is also the quarterback with the most division titles to his name after having helped the Patriots win the AFC East crown 14 times, so far.

In addition to being one of the best quarterbacks in NFL history, Brady has also been able to the benefit of leading some great offensive units during his time as well. Brady has led offenses that have scored 50 or more points in eight separate games in his career, the most of any quarterback. The most recent were the 51 points the Patriots scored against the Jacksonville Jaguars on September 27, 2015. Concerning the most points he has ever scored – it is a tie between the 59 he scored against the Tennessee Titans on October 18, 2009, and the 59 points scored against the Indianapolis Colts on November 18, 2012. Brady's biggest playoff success came during the dynasty years in 2001 and between 2003 and 2005 where Brady had the longest postseason winning streak with ten wins.

That postseason success has continued into the Super Bowl, where Brady has played seven times for the NFL's Vince Lombardi Trophy – a league record.

Those numbers go along with his impressive 5-2 record in the Super Bowl, making him the most decorated quarterback in Super Bowl history ahead of Montana (XVI, XIX, XXIII, and XXIV) with the San Francisco 49ers and Terry Bradshaw (IX, X, XIII, and XIV) with the Pittsburgh Steelers.[xliii] Although both of those Hall of Fame quarterbacks never lost a Super Bowl game, Brady has two defeats to the younger Manning brother, Eli, and the New York Giants in Super Bowl XLII in 2008 and Super Bowl XLVI in 2012. But with three more years of his newly extended contract with the Patriots and the team having salary cap flexibility, the odds are in favor of Brady possibly picking up a ring that would go on his other hand to mark a sixth title.

Chapter 12: Outside of Football

Part of being one of the greatest quarterbacks in the world's most famous sports associations means getting a chance to do many different things, along with some celebrity status. One of Brady's earliest examples was an opportunity to host an episode of Saturday Night Live in 2005.[xliv] He talked about how he is used to performing well under pressure in front of millions of football fans, so he had a monologue where he focused on showing off his other talents like singing while surrounded by a group of the SNL cast members. In addition to signing, Brady also showed some skills with dancing, completing the crossword puzzle in the New York Times, and the ability to speak Japanese. There was also some humor shown as he jokingly claimed that he won the Tour de France without any pants and that he was able to kill a horse with his bare hands. Part of being the host of Saturday Night Live means being able to perform in a number sketches where he struggled to get a football through a target at a carnival, something that can be done by others without any issues. People around the country started to learn that Brady knew how to be funny and that he was not just some jock quarterback that did not have any personality – and that he also loved funnel cake.

In addition to being able to act in live comedy sketches, Brady has also lent his voice to a few iconic cartoons. The first was aired in a February 2005 episode of the Simpsons aired shortly after Brady and the New England Patriots defeated the Philadelphia Eagles, 24-21.

The episode was based on Homer Simpson's embarrassing victory dance becoming a trend where several sports stars are recruiting him to help them with their victory dance – including a cartoon version of Brady riding down the field on a scooter with a banner that says "everybody sucks but me." While many sports purists hate the new dances, it even led to Homer being asked to choreograph the halftime show for the Super Bowl. It was a very brief voice spot in the cartoon, but the episode gained some huge ratings with a total of about 23.1 million people watching the original broadcast on Super Bowl Sunday. It was sixth overall for the week with the Super Bowl game finishing first overall.[xlv] Still, not bad for a cartoon show.

However, Brady would top that with an extended role in an episode of Fox's Family Guy in 2006 called "Patriot Games."[xlvi] The episode started with the lead character, Peter Griffin, making an attempt to make his former classmates attending his high school reunion think he was a big shot by describing himself as a "secret agent-astronaut-millionaire," while wearing a cowboy hat, in front of one of his friends who brought Brady. After being caught in his lie, Griffin gets drunk and makes a run to the restroom. Having pushed several people out of the way, Brady recruits Griffin to play on the offensive line of the Patriots; a dream come true for Griffin who has lived in the New England area (specifically Rhode Island) his entire life. There is a clash of personalities that lead to Brady firing Griffin and he forming a football team in England to challenge the Patriots – basically not going so well for Griffin. It was a memorable episode where Brady

117

held a very long role with plenty of funny one-liners and exchanges with the Family Guy regulars, once again adding to the public opinion that Brady is more than just someone who throws a football for millions of dollars.

That relationship between Brady and Family Guy creator and writer Seth McFarland continued in 2015 when the Patriots' quarterback made a brief cameo in the movie Ted 2. Mark Wahlberg and his best friend, a teddy bear that came to life by a child's wish, attempted to try to get a sample of Brady so that Ted's girlfriend can have a child who has an almost guaranteed future in football. They need a donor because the teddy bear cannot have a child. The trailer was shown during the Super Bowl in February 2015. Once Brady wakes up, he tosses the two out of the second floor of his house and Ted, the bear, out the window like a football into the arms of Wahlberg's character. By the way, Wahlberg comments that the throw was a perfect spiral, which should not be a surprise to anyone who has followed Brady's career in the NFL.

Additionally, Brady made brief cameos in a 2009 episode of Entourage and then in the 2015 film adaptation for a group of friends involved in the world of sports agents. Overall, Brady has been able to receive many opportunities where he has been given some exposure in film and television that just builds overall fame for a quarterback who deserved the attention. One cannot deny that Brady has many skills and will hopefully be involved in television after his football career ends. What is more likely to happen is that he could be a football analyst on a major network, like many football players do after they retire for the NFL. At the same time, we hope he gets involved in some more television and movie projects, maybe if there is a third Ted movie or another comedy that can include football – like a football sitcom on Fox or CBS? Regardless, Brady should have no trouble being able to find work when he does retire. He has shown since the voiceover on the Simpsons and hosting Saturday Night Live in 2005 that he is comfortable being in front of a camera for more than just a post-game conference after a big game or tough loss on the football field.

Chapter 13: Brady's Personal Life

During the height of Brady's popularity, he was dating Hollywood actress Bridget Moynahan starting in 2004. The New England quarterback was seen at multiple red carpet events with Moynahan, who was about six years Brady's elder and was one of multiple television roles that included Sex and the City, where she played the socialite wife of the character Mr. Big. The relationship continued for three years until December 2006[xlvii]. But that was not the end of their story, because around the time they announced their splitting up, Moynahan was announced to be pregnant with Brady's child. The two never got back together, but Brady was present on the day of his son's birth in August 2007 at Saint John's Health Center near Brady's hometown in Santa Monica, California; granted he was not in the delivery room with Moynahan.[xlviii] The boy was named John Edward Thomas Moynahan. Now, just because they were not dating did not mean they were not working together to raise the child in a healthy family, even when Brady was dating someone else. In fact, during an interview with People Magazine, Moynahan stated that she was still working with Brady and his current wife Gisele Bundchen as part of a blended family that has made being a single mom a little bit easier.

About a month after splitting up from Moynahan, Brady was starting to be seen with the model everyone refers to by the first name Gisele, although reports were that they started dating just before Christmas in 2006.[xlix] At first, sources close to the situation were telling the media the news while Brady would not comment. Shortly after the Brazilian-born model had broken up with actor Leonardo DiCaprio in 2005, she had mentioned that she thought Brady was not too shabby and was cute in an All-American way, but the interview stated that at the time, Brady was dating Moynahan and she considers men who are with someone as off-limits. But reports were that the two had met through a mutual friend, and the rumors started to become bigger when there were reports that the model was seen outside the Patriots locker room after a game on January 14, 2007, against the San Diego Chargers.

For about two years, people were talking about the power couple that almost resembled a high school romance – the superstar from the football field in Brady, and arguably one of the most beautiful women in Bundchen. It seemed like a relationship that was working out well, especially when the news broke that the two got married sometime around February 2007 after getting engaged in January 2007, according to sources close to Brady and Bundchen.[l] It was a very private ceremony held at St. Monica Catholic Church in Santa Monica, California, and only a select group of people were invited to the ceremony. One of the notable people in attendance was his son John Edward Thomas, who was just 18 months old at the time, and was likely with his mother Moynahan – Brady's ex-girlfriend. There was a second ceremony that was held in Costa Rica a few months later with photographs being posted by the bride on her social media accounts only recently as Bundchen's contribution to the weekly "Throwback Thursday" tradition as part of celebrating their anniversary.[li]

Since they became a married couple, the two have had two children, with the first being a boy they named Benjamin Rein Brady in December 2009, although the couple did admit there was some struggle finding a perfect name for their baby boy and that they decided on Benjamin about ten days after his arrival.[lii] About three years later in December 2012, the couple would welcome their second child, a daughter they named Vivian Lake Brady, while they were at their home in Boston, giving the NFL star quarterback three children in total.[liii] The family has lived in luxury because of the lucrative incomes from a quarterback dad and a supermodel mom. The family spent most of their time residing in a mansion in the Brentwood section of Los Angeles that was worth about $20 million. The family then purchased and moved into a condominium worth about $14 million located at One Madison in Manhattan, New York. The family is awaiting the construction of a brand new home closer to Boston, Massachusetts, which should be completed very soon.

Usually, there has been a prevailing thought that the husband and father of the household would customarily bring in the income – or as the adage would go, he would "bring home the bacon." In 2015, Brady had made about $31.3 million in his contract and winnings from the NFL season and then another $7 million for some endorsement deals from various companies and brand names.[liv] At the same time, his wife Gisele has made a lot more money in total with about $44 million made in 2015; thanks to having a part in some major fashion campaigns with big names like Emilio Pucci.[lv] Granted, it probably does not bother the NFL quarterback since both he and his wife are currently enjoying their careers while being able to help their children have a bright, financial future. It should not matter where the money is coming from.

On a side note about Brady's personal life, his sister Julie married another well-known athlete that sports fans in Boston and the rest of the Northeast region of the United States love – Kevin Youkilis, who spent most of his 10-year career in Major League Baseball with the Boston Red Sox. After Youkilis had divorced his first wife, he had dated Brady's sister Julie for about a year before proposing to the sister who is now a schoolteacher[lvi]. But two of Boston's top sports stars from the past decade are brothers-in-law, both helping the city of Boston win multiple championships within the 2000s decade between the New England Patriots and the Boston Red Sox.

Chapter 14: Brady's Charitable Work

Brady's wife Gisele has been named incredibly generous with $1.5 million given to relief efforts in Haiti, another $1 million for people suffering from the aftermath of the Tohoku earthquakes in Japan, and many foundations helping cancer research, hurricane victims, and empowering young girls.[lvii] But Brady himself has made many charitable contributions, which include helping Best Buddies International continue to raise money to help people who have mental and developmental conditions and disabilities through partnerships with friends and mentors. Brady has done this through donating nearly $200,000 towards the fee that he usually charges for speaking at an event while also coordinating a challenge where the winning donor to the cause can take part in a touch football game with Brady.

One of Brady's more recent charitable donations was in the amount $50,000 to the Jimmy Fun radio-telethon between Boston's NESN and WEEI, a charity that helps raise money for helping adult and child cancer patients with care and benefits from continued cancer research.[lviii] This was actually money that was expected to go towards a fine to the NFL regarding the problems that arose from Brady's supposed role in what was called Deflate-Gate. However, that was a fake story that made the rounds and was later debunked by Mike Florio of NBC Sports' Pro Football Talk.

Some of the other charities that Brady has worked with also includes the Boys and Girls Clubs of America, the Entertainment Industry

Foundation, and KaBoom!, an organization that focuses on providing playground and other outdoor activities and equipment for children living in neighborhoods in need. Brady is one of the several professional athletes who have made an effort to give back to people through the money he has made in his athletic career.

Chapter 15: Tom Brady's Legacy

While there has been a lot of controversy surrounding Tom Brady and his legacy, there is no denying what the man has done on the football field as one of the greatest quarterbacks, not only within this generation, but of all-time. Currently, Brady holds a record of 5-2 in Super Bowl games. He leads all quarterbacks in the NFL with a total of seven appearances, with John Elway in second with five (2-3). Brady is one of two players in NFL history to have five championships and the only quarterback to lead a team to five Super Bowl titles.

While Montana and Bradshaw won a combined eight Super Bowl games without a loss, one could imagine Brady's legacy had those two losses to the Giants had never happened. A victory in Super Bowl XLII would have resulted in just the second perfect season in NFL history, and the first 19-0 record by a team. Considering the consistent seasons with double-digit victory totals and the ability to attract key free agent players, it is likely the New England Patriots will make at least one more championship run before Brady retires.

Brady will probably be one of only a few quarterbacks play beyond the golden age of 40. The older a quarterback ages, the more their performances decline, based on information accumulated by Football Perspective's article on the age curves of quarterbacks. Then again, quarterbacks like Brady and Peyton Manning have maintained a higher value through the years and gradually regressed, unlike the average quarterback who might not remain in the league that long. It is a challenge just to remain in a league where there are only 53 roster spots to start the season. There are always younger stars entering from college every spring in the NFL Draft and a number of talented arms looking for a chance to make an immediate impact for the clubs that select them.

Even if Brady does not add a sixth Super Bowl title, he is a sure-fire first-ballot Hall of Fame player. Despite the controversies, there is not enough proof to claim that all of his career numbers are marred – numbers that will compose the resume to be included with the league's greatest legends. Voters usually look at what is accomplished on the field, unless there is evidence that places a black mark on a player's record. These marks could include failed drug tests, documents supporting the accusations, etc. Brady has had none of that on his record, and, as things currently stand, he should be a first-ballot nomination to have his likeness enshrined in Canton, Ohio.

After signing a contract extension with the Patriots in March 2016 means that he is going to play three more seasons through the 2019 NFL season, Brady has the potential to reach 70,000 passing yards and 500 touchdowns. There were only three seasons when Brady did not play all 16 games of a regular season – his rookie year in 2000 when he had one appearance behind Drew Bledsoe, the 2008 season when he was injured in the opening game of the season against the Kansas City Chiefs and of course, his suspension-shortened 2016 campaign. Other than those three seasons, Brady has not missed a start and currently has a streak of 124 starts as a quarterback.

Among those numbers, Brady holds the NFL record for most passing touchdowns in a season with 50 in 2007, which topped Peyton Manning's 49 in 2004 and Dan Marino's 48 in 1984. Depending on Brees' longevity as well as Brady's ability to stay healthy, it is very possible Brady could finish his career as the NFL's all-time leader in passing yards and touchdown passes.

Favre's numbers were accumulated from playing for a total of 20 seasons between four different teams, although he is most noted for his time with the Green Bay Packers. Favre was also more of a gunslinger than Brady has been.

Then again, Brady has always strived on achieving ambitious goals, and he has a pretty good track record of doing what many never expected. Just like some people doubted he would be the better athlete in the Brady household and also when people saw that he chose to play collegiate football at the University of Michigan. There were also doubts when he entered the NFL Draft and waited a long time until the sixth round before New England picked him up in 2000. Behind Bledsoe and a few other men on the depth chart, how was it possible for Brady to get the time to be noticed?

Beyond that, how would someone who was a second-year player come off the bench with only a few throws to his name fit into Bill Belichick's offensive game plan when Bledsoe went down with an injury in 2001? Well, that second-year player was able to grow in the system that had one of the scrappiest defenses in the league and with a dominant running game, not to mention having who would become one of the league's most clutch field goal kickers of all-time. A few years later, Brady would win three more Super Bowls after being that sixth-round draft pick and someone a lot of NFL scouts did not put a lot of stock into when he was leaving the campus in Ann Arbor, Michigan. Brady had the drive at a young age to prove people wrong, and it has shown to hold firm even to today when he continues to post incredible numbers every season and will have a good chance to become the highest rated quarterback in NFL history with both statistics and championship rings to back that claim up.

Sure, some people think he is someone who might not have to prove anything and that he did not need to win that fifth Super Bowl ring to be considered the best. Combine the people who make those claims with those who believe that Brady might not have a whole lot left in the gas tank, or air in the tires, to play another three seasons. If there is anything that football fans and experts should have learned by now is that Brady seems to be the type of athlete that strives to perform against the doubt and the criticism to go along with the drive to be the best that anyone has ever seen. Brady is a lot like the best professional athletes in other sports, more so like Michael Jordan, who won six championships with the Chicago Bulls during the 1990s. While Brady is only aiming for five titles to be the all-time winningest quarterback concerning Super Bowl rings, there is a good chance he could always seek to set that bar higher than anyone ever thought was possible. However, it seems like Brady will always have a source of motivation from some direction of the NFL fan base.

Final Word/About the Author

I was born and raised in Norwalk, Connecticut. Growing up, I could often be found spending many nights watching basketball, soccer, and football matches with my father in the family living room. I love sports and everything that sports can embody. I believe that sports are one of most genuine forms of competition, heart, and determination. I write my works to learn more about influential athletes in the hopes that from my writing, you the reader can walk away inspired to put in an equal if not greater amount of hard work and perseverance to pursue your goals. If you enjoyed *Tom Brady*, please leave a review! Also, you can read more of my works on *Roger Federer, Novak Djokovic, Andrew Luck, Rob Gronkowski, Brett Favre, Calvin Johnson, Drew Brees, J.J. Watt, Colin Kaepernick, Aaron Rodgers, Peyton Manning, Russell Wilson, Michael Jordan, LeBron James, Kyrie Irving, Klay Thompson, Stephen Curry, Kevin Durant, Russell Westbrook, Anthony Davis, Chris Paul, Blake Griffin, Kobe Bryant, Joakim Noah, Scottie Pippen, Carmelo Anthony, Kevin Love, Grant Hill, Tracy McGrady, Vince Carter, Patrick Ewing, Karl Malone, Tony Parker, Allen Iverson, Hakeem Olajuwon, Reggie Miller, Michael Carter-Williams, John Wall, James Harden, Tim Duncan, Steve Nash, Draymond Green, Kawhi Leonard, Dwyane Wade, Ray Allen, Pau Gasol, Dirk Nowitzki, Jimmy Butler, Paul Pierce, Manu Ginobili, Pete Maravich, Larry Bird, Kyle Lowry, Jason Kidd, David Robinson, LaMarcus Aldridge, Derrick Rose, Paul George, Kevin Garnett, Chris Paul, Marc Gasol, Yao Ming, Al Horford, Amar'e*

Stoudemire, DeMar DeRozan, Isaiah Thomas, Kemba Walker and Chris Bosh in the Kindle Store. If you love football, check out my website at claytongeoffreys.com to join my exclusive list where I let you know about my latest books and give you lots of goodies.

Like what you read? Please leave a review!

I write because I love sharing the stories of influential people like Tom Brady with fantastic readers like you. My readers inspire me to write more so please do not hesitate to let me know what you thought by leaving a review! If you love books on life, football, or productivity, check out my website at claytongeoffreys.com to join my exclusive list where I let you know about my latest books. Aside from being the first to hear about my latest releases, you can also download a free copy of *33 Life Lessons: Success Principles, Career Advice & Habits of Successful People*. See you there!

Clayton

References

[i] "Tom Brady rebounds as Pats punish Raiders for many mistakes." *ESPN.com.* ESPN Internet Services

[ii] "Joe Montana" *Sports-Reference.com.* Sports Reference, LLC. N.d. Web.

[iii] Ducibella, Jim. "W&M's football facilities growing." *Highbeam.com.* Virginia Pilot and Ledger-Star. 28 June 2005. Web.

[iv] Cimini, Rich. "Story of boy named Tom Brady." *NYDailyNews.com.* New York Daily News. 25 January 2008. Web.

[v] "2004 Athletic Hall of Fame Inductees." *SerraHS.com.* Junipero Serra High School. 27 September 2007. Web.

[vi] Garber, Greg. "The Tom Brady Experience: 'Almost' perfect." *ESPN.com.* ESPN Internet Ventures. 1 February 2008. Web.

[vii] Garber, Greg. "The Tom Brady Experience: 'Almost' perfect." *ESPN.com.* ESPN Internet Ventures. 1 February 2008. Web.

[viii] Kirpalani, Sanjay. "The College Recruitment of Tom Brady." *BleacherReport.com.* Bleacher Report. 24 September 2015. Web.

[ix] Garber, Greg. "The Tom Brady Experience: 'Almost' perfect." *ESPN.com.* ESPN Internet Ventures. 1 February 2008. Web.

[x] "1995 Michigan Wolverines Stats." *Sports-Reference.com.* Sports Reference, LLC. N.d. Web.

[xi] Garber, Greg. "The Tom Brady Experience: 'Almost' perfect." *ESPN.com.* ESPN Internet Ventures. 1 February 2008. Web.

[xii] "Tom Brady." *Sports-Reference.com.* Sports Reference, LLC. N.d. Web.

[xiii] "Carr Names Brady as Wolverines' Top Quarterback." *MGoBlue*.com. University of Michigan. N.d. Web.

[xiv] "Michigan Rallies for 45-31 Citrus Bowl Win over Arkansas. *MGoBlue*.com. University of Michigan. N.d. Web.

[xv] Nesbitt, Stephen J. "Teammates Reflect on Tom Brady-Drew Henson Battle, David Terrell's Rise to Fame." *The Michigan Daily.* 31 August 2012. Web.

[xvi] "Tom Brady's Top Three Games as a Wolverine." MGoBlue.com. University of Michigan. 16 September 2010. Web.

[xvii] "Tom Brady's Top Three Games as a Wolverine." MGoBlue.com.

University of Michigan. 16 September 2010. Web.

[xviii] "Tom Brady's Top Three Games as a Wolverine." MGoBlue.com. University of Michigan. 16 September 2010. Web.

[xix] "Tom Brady's college resume." *ESPN.com*. ESPN Internet Ventures. 29 November 2014. Web.

[xx] Game notes and statistics from "Tom Brady." *Pro-Football-Reference.com*. Sports Reference, LLC. N.d. Web.

[xxi] "1999 NFL Draft – Round 1." *NFL.com*. National Football League. N.d. Web.

[xxii] "Tom Brady." *Pro-Football Reference.com*. Sports Reference, LLC. N.d. Web.

[xxiii] Cafardo, Nick. "Drew Bledsoe hurt as 0-2 Patriots lose to Jets." *BostonGlobe.com*. Boston Globe. 24 September 2001. Web.

[xxiv] Caesar, Dan. "14-Point Spread Isn't About Respect." *STLouisToday*.com. St. Louis Post-Dispatch. 30 January 2002. Web.

[xxv] Game notes and statistics from "Tom Brady." *Pro-Football-Reference.com*. Sports Reference, LLC. N.d. Web.

[xxvi] Benne, Jon. "A look back at the Panthers' first Super Bowl appearance." *SBNation.com*. Vox Media, Inc. 7 Feb. 2016. Web.

[xxvii] "Vinatieri the hero, Brady the MVP." *ESPN.com*. ESPN Internet Ventures. 4 February 2004. Web.

[xxviii] "Investigative Report Concerning Footballs Used During the AFC Championship on January 18, 2015." *NFL.com*. National Football League. 6 May 2015. Web.

[xxix] Rosenthal, Gregg. "Tom Brady suspended four games, plans to appeal." *NFL.com*. National Football League. 12 May 2015. Web.

[xxx] "NFL releases statement on Patriots' violations." *NFL.com*. National Football League. 11 May 2015. Web.

[xxxi] Patra, Kevin. "Tom Brady appeals suspension; Goodell to hear case." *NFL.com*. National Football League. 15 May 2015. Web.

[xxxii] "NFL upholds four-game suspension of Tom Brady." *CBSNews.com*. CBS News. 28 July 2015. Web.

[xxxiii] Cole, Mike. "Report: Tom Brady Authorizes NFLPA to Appeal His Case in Federal Court." *NESN.com*. New England Sports Network. 28 July 2015. Web.

[xxxiv] Kerr-Dineen, Luke. "Tom Brady rips the NFL's Deflategate decision on his Facebook page." FTW.USAToday.com. USA Today.

29 July 2015. Web.

[xxxv] Belson, Ken. "Judge erases Tom Brady's suspension; NFL says it will appeal." *NYTimes.com*. New York Times. 3 September 2015. Web.

[xxxvi] Game notes and statistics from "Tom Brady." *Pro-Football-Reference.com*. Sports Reference, LLC. N.d. Web.

[xxxvii] Wilson, Ryan. "Tom Brady breaks Brett Favre's record for most wins with one team." *CBSSports.com*. CBS Sports. 11 September 2015. Web.

[xxxviii] "C.J. Anderson scampers 48 yards for TD to ruin Pats' unblemished record." *ESPN.com*. ESPN Internet Ventures. 30 November 2015. Web.

[xxxix] Reiss, Mike. "New deal links Tom Brady to Patriots through 2019." *ESPN.com*. ESPN Internet Services. 29 February 2016. Web.

[xl] Schlager, Brandon. "Deflategate returns: Everything to know about NFL's upcoming appeal." *SportingNews.com*. Sporting News. 29 February 2016. Web.

[xli] McCann, Michael. "Track records of judges who'll decide NFL's Deflategate appeal." *SI.com*. Sports Illustrated. 25 February 2016. Web.

[xlii] "NFL History – Passing Yardage Leaders." *ESPN.com*. ESPN Internet Ventures. N.d. Web.

[xliii] "Tom Brady ties record for most Super Bowl wins by a quarterback." *SI.com*. Sports Illustrated. 1 February 2015. Web.

[xliv] "Monologue: Tom Brady Shows Off His Other Talents." *NBC.com/SaturdayNightLive*. NBC. 16 April 2005. Web.

[xlv] Saunders, Dusty. "Nielsen Ratings." *STLToday.com*. St. Louis Post-Dispatch. 11 February 2005. Web.

[xlvi] "Family Guy 'Patriot Games.'" *IMDB.com*. Internet Movie Database. N.d. Web.

[xlvii] Dagostino, Mark. "Tom Brady, Bridget Moynahan Split Up." *People.com*. People Magazine. 14 December 2006. Web.

[xlviii] Hammel, Sara. "Bridget Moynahan Maintains a 'Loving' Family for Son with Ex Tom Brady." People.com. People Magazine. 22 February 2011

[xlix] "Tom Brady and Gisele Bundchen: New Couple?" *People.com*. People Magazine. 25 January 2007. Web.

[l] Cedenheim, Pernilla. "Tom Brady & Gisel Bundchen Get Married!" *People.com*. People Magazine. 27 February 2009. Web.
[li] Martin, Annie. "Gisele Bundchen shares wedding photo with Tom Brady." *UPI.com*. United Press International. 27 February 2015. Web.
[lii] Griffin, Bauer. "Gisele Bundchen and Tom Brady Name Son Benjamin." *People.com*. People Magazine. 10 March 2010. Web.
[liii] "Gisele Bundchen and Tom Brady Welcome Daughter Vivian Lake." *People.com*. People Magazine. 7 December 2012. Web.
[liv] "Tom Brady." *Forbes.com*. Forbes Magazine. N.d. Web.
[lv] "Gisele Bundchen." *Forbes.com*. Forbes Magazine. N.d. Web.
[lvi] Farrar, Doug. "Boston (in) Common: Kevin Youkilis set to marry Tom Brady's sister." *Sports.yahoo.com*. Yahoo. 10 February 2012.
[lvii] "8 Surprisingly Charitable Celebrities." *Smosh.com*. Smosh. 2014. Web.
[lviii] Florio, Mike. "Tom Brady gives $50,000 to the Jimmy Fund." *ProFootballTalk*.com. NBC Sports. 19 August 2015.

Made in the USA
San Bernardino, CA
23 July 2018